Anthropology:
Weaving Our Discipline
with Community

Anthropology:
Weaving Our Discipline
with Community

Edited by

Lisa J. Lefler

Selected Papers from the Annual Meeting of the
Southern Anthropological Society,
Cherokee, North Carolina,
March 30–April 1, 2014

Betty J. Duggan
SAS Proceedings Interim Series Editor

Newfound Press
THE UNIVERSITY OF TENNESSEE LIBRARIES, KNOXVILLE

Southern Anthropological Society
Founded 1966

Anthropology: Weaving Our Discipline with Community
© 2020 by Southern Anthropological Society: *southernanthro.org*

Print on demand available through University of Tennessee Press.
DOI: *https://doi.org/10.7290/akiz914*

For all other uses, contact:
Newfound Press
University of Tennessee Libraries
1015 Volunteer Boulevard
Knoxville, TN 37996-1000
newfoundpress.utk.edu

ISBN-13: 978-0-9860803-8-8 (paperback)
ISBN-13: 978-0-9860803-9-5 (PDF)

Names: Lefler, Lisa J., editor, contributor, writer of introduction. | Hudson, Charles
    M., dedicatee, [and 5 others]. | Southern Anthropological Society. Meeting (2014 :
    Cherokee, NC)
Title: Anthropology : weaving our discipline with community / edited by Lisa J. Lefler.
Description: Knoxville, Tennessee : Newfound Press, University of Tennessee Libraries,
    [2020] | 1 online resource | Series: Southern Anthropological Society proceedings ;
    no. 45. | Includes bibliographical references. | Summary: "Selected Papers from
    the Annual Meeting of the Southern Anthropological Society, Cherokee, North
    Carolina, March 30–April 1, 2014."
Subjects: LCSH: University of North Carolina at Asheville—Congresses. | Eastern Band
    of Cherokee Indians—Congresses. | Cherokee Indians—North Carolina, Western—
    Congresses. | Cherokee Indians—Health and hygiene—Eastern Band of Cherokee
    Indians—Congresses. | Traditional medicine—Eastern Band of Cherokee Indians—
    Congresses. | Cherokee language—Preservation—Methodology—Congresses. |
    Indians of North America—Education (Higher)—North Carolina—Asheville—
    Case studies—Congresses. | Community organization—North Carolina, Western—
    Case studies—Congresses. | Ethnology—Fieldwork—Eastern Band of Cherokee
    Indians—Cross-cultural studies—Congresses. | Ethnology—Fieldwork—Guinea-
    Bissau—Cross-cultural studies—Congresses. | Anthropology—Southern States—
    Methodology—Congresses.
Classification: LCC GN2.S68 no.45eb (PDF) | LCC GN2.S68 no.45 (print)

Book design by Martha Rudolph
Cover design by C. S. Jenkins

Contents

Introduction

Lisa J. Lefler

For many people, anthropology is a mystical or even marginal discipline. Most often people think of anthropologists as merely archaeologists who dig up the past or, even more specifically, paleoanthropologists who spend their careers piecing together giant bones and fossils of animals from the prehistoric past. I hope this volume creates a fuller appreciation among those who don't know much about what we do or who may see us in a negative light, thinking we only go into communities to exploit them for knowledge. A popular *Far Side* cartoon by Gary Larson comes to mind. It pictures three "native" people inside a hut. One looks out the window at two figures headed their way with notebook and camera in hand and shouts Anthropologists! Anthropologists! while the other two occupants bustle their television, telephone, lamp, and VCR from the hut. Instead of being an annoyance to people, we hope in this volume to provide more positive examples of our lifelong efforts to preserve, conserve, protect, and perpetuate the dynamic and rich cultures of communities. We hope we can shed light on problems that have troubled humanity in the past as well as offering practical suggestions for the future.

Anthropologists work on practically every issue that humanity has encountered. What allows us to engage in this massive undertaking is the way in which anthropology is organized. Our discipline is divided into four major subfields: biological or physical anthropology, linguistic anthropology, socio-cultural anthropology, and archaeology. Each of these four subfields has many sub-subfields, each garnering a more specific focus on some activity or study of humankind. For instance, you can have a concentration in socio-cultural anthropology and also specialize in education, ethno-history, or medicine cross-culturally. You can have a concentration in physical anthropology but specialize in forensics or primatology. But the real bonus and wonderful nature of anthropology is that in our study of human activity we have cross-training to some degree in all subfields, providing us with multiple lenses and tools with which to work, as we emphasize working with others, collaboration, and fieldwork.

Anthropologists have extensive experience in working across disciplines with other professionals to tackle problems. We were, in a very real sense, the initiators of multi-cultural studies and diversity training. Some of the earliest scholarship and research on gender and race, for example, came from anthropologists who were studying in communities all over the world. For example, it was from early anthropological field studies and the likes of Franz Boas and Margaret Mead that we came to understand that race and gender are social—not biological—constructs. Through the work of anthropologists we came to understand that our health and behavior are a result of both biology *and* environment, nature *and* nurture—not just one *or* the other. The dynamic contemporary science of epigenetics is proving that both DNA and environment are important in being able to understand and predict chronic disease. Epigenetics depends on those working in the medical and social sciences putting their heads and theories together for a better, fuller understanding of humans and health. From these contemporary theories we gain a better understanding of just how our history and environment impacts population health and health inter-generationally.

But I think our most important and effective strategy is our deep commitment and devotion to working with and in communities. Without community assistance, buy-in, and support, we could not do what we do—or at least do what we do with any effectiveness. Most anthropologists have focused on two important research strategies that have historically set us apart from other disciplines: (1) qualitative research methods and (2) community-engaged research strategies, now often referred to as CBPR (Community-Based Participatory Research). Because socio-cultural anthropologists were required to do fieldwork in and with the people they were studying, there had to be a human connection made to the people who were helping with language, customs, and other daily activities that allowed anthropologists to do their work. Eventually, after decades of mistakes and lessons learned, we were able to develop more positive strategies to gain the trust and respect necessary for effective research cross-culturally.

Today, those of us who work with tribal communities understand that our work depends, foremost, on our positive relationship and mutual respect for those with whom we work. Instead of CBPR, it sometimes is referred to as TBPR, Tribally-Based Participatory Research. Tribal people must be full partners in initiating the research, gain the greatest benefit of the research, and be integral participants and drivers in the research. Their input and initiation are critical to any work conducted in Native communities. If it is not of benefit to the community, it should not be done—plain and simple. Several years ago, a Tribal health administrator for the Eastern Band of Cherokee Indians, in a meeting about research, spoke the simple phrase, "nothing about us, without us," and I have never forgotten the importance of that short and concise saying.

The focus of the 2014 SAS conference and of this volume is *how* anthropology works with communities. We wanted scholars and students to show from our different lenses and subfields how we weave our activities with those of the communities with whom we work, for a broader understanding of issues. Excerpting from the program:

> As we move into the 21st Century we can draw upon our holistic discipline to examine topics ranging from climate change to language death. The Cherokee basket watermarked in our 49th annual program is exemplary of how skilled hands can weave multiple types of materials and patterns to create a single outcome that successfully reflects heritage, meaning, and purpose. Coming back to a four-field discipline provides stronger resources to meet our purpose of understanding the human experience.

This volume provides the ethnographic stories of early work with the Eastern Band of Cherokee Indians, as well as more recent work with this community. Ray Fogelson, who has mentored many of us in Cherokee studies, provides a glimpse of his very important work beginning in the late 1950s and early 1960s, while linguist Hartwell Francis shares his work on language preservation in the community today. The last two chapters by Jim Sarbaugh and myself, focusing on traditional knowledge and health, also reflect many years of work regarding the Cherokee. Trey Adcock, a Native educator, while not an anthropologist, works in Native studies and shows the importance of interdisciplinary work in providing an effective and vibrant program in a university on Cherokee homeland. Brandon Lundy's chapter provides insight into ethnographic methodology and uses his work in Guinea-Bissau to demonstrate the process of partnering to produce data that provides real knowledge about people and community.

We hope that this manuscript is useful for those interested in working with communities—particularly those communities that have been colonized—by providing more effective perspectives and approaches to conducting partnered research for the benefit of the community.

Tradition: Intermittent and Persistent, with Particular Reference to the Cherokees[1]

Raymond D. Fogelson

There seems to be little disagreement on the definition of tradition. Disputes only arise with respect to the value of tradition, its significance and authenticity. As a starting point, a definition of tradition found in the *Encyclopedia Britannica* will suffice: "an aggregate of custom, beliefs and practices that give continuity to a culture, civilization and social group and thus shape its views."

Etymologically, the word "tradition" derives from the Latin *tradere* —"to hand over, deliver." A related secondary meaning refers to "giving up," "surrender," and "betrayed"—and surprisingly is the root of the term "treason."

Tradition implies an oral transmission from generation to generation of opinions, doctrines, practices, rites, and customs. The Ten Commandments of Moses were passed on orally before being inscribed in stone; core Christian doctrines were kept alive through oral transmission before being written down long after Christ's crucifixion. For Muslims, the printed Koran is surrounded by and dependent upon a large body of oral tradition.

For some thinkers, tradition is less a continuous connection to a glorified past and more an impediment to progress and social improvement. Henry Ford is famous for his judgment that "history is bunk." (Parenthetically, the word "bunk" originates from the perorations of an infamous member of the House of Representatives from nearby Buncombe County, North Carolina.) However, it is worth returning to Ford's fuller exclamation. He said:

> History is more or less bunk. It's tradition. We don't want tradition. We want to live in the present and the only history that is worth a tinker's damn is the history that we make today.

For Ford, tradition can be dismissed as an irritant, a cuticle hanging precariously on the dead hand of history. Tradition thus is antiquarian, anti-modern, backward-looking and highly romantic. There is a strong irony here: the same Ford whose assembly lines[2] accelerated the American Industrial miracle that transformed our cultural landscape also was a prime mover behind the restoration of Colonial Williamsburg, as well as the founding of Michigan's Greenfield Village, a romanticized version of pre-Industrial America. Indeed, tradition be damned.

The idea of tradition has drawn its share of ambivalent skepticism. In his justly forgotten film *Deconstructing Harry*, Woody Allen remarks, "Tradition is the illusion of permanence." The reality and authenticity of tradition has been challenged by Eric Hobsbawm and Terence Ranger, with their notion of invented traditions. Invented traditions possess shallow time depth and dubious origins. Invented traditions often lend themselves to commodification in their capacity for objectification. So-called "real traditions" have more blurred boundaries and indeterminate, drifting timelines. Yet all traditions, whether real, invented, or re-invented, require social recognition. Today's event may become tomorrow's tradition.

A more positive approach views traditions as akin to notions of collective identity. This refers not only to a unifying collective self-image, projected both outward and inward, but also to a process of temporal continuity and sameness. My friend Robert McKinley insightfully refers to this process as cultural self-awareness. Cultural self-awareness implies a critical and semi-objective sense of one's own culture. Long ago, Paul Radin argued that every society contained a small number of thinkers who questioned the everyday assumptions of its general populace and constructed new philosophical systems. It was also Radin who showed that Native skepticism was evident in the mythic behavior of trickster figures. Tricksters violated social convention and pushed cultural understanding to its limits, thereby making manifest cultural self-awareness.

The tension between Native philosophers and true believers in every society provides the spark that gives vitality to tradition. However, the life careers of traditions can take some tricky turns. Traditions may often cease to be protected, but their memories may persist in a latent state of abeyance.

At the right moment the tradition may re-emerge either full-blown or in a revised form. The Kwakwa'wakw resumed potlatching fifty years after its legal prohibition. Descendants remembered who owed what to whom. In 1958, I witnessed Big Cove ballplayers form two parallel lines for war cries of the *talala*, or pileated woodpecker. They repeated the ritual four times, each time advancing a few feet. This was a condensed version of the ancient war path ritual. After the performance, the ballplayers departed by pickup truck for an exhibition game in Cherokee.

Our contemporary political scene has witnessed the emergence of the Tea Party. This conservative group of anti-big government, super-patriots takes its cue from the tax revolt by a mob of protesters unconvincingly disguised from head to toe as Mohawks. They riotously dumped a large shipment of English tea into Boston Harbor on December 16, 1773. This, of course, was seen as a prelude to the American Revolution—or Rebellion, depending on which side of the Atlantic you came from. Interestingly, as historian Alfred

Young documents in his fascinating book *The Shoemaker and the Tea Party*, the event didn't become known as the Boston Tea Party until almost 50 years later. Young makes an important distinction between private memory (what an individual remembers about an event he or she has experienced or observed) and public memory ("what a society remembers collectively, or after most private memories have faded or disappeared, the way it constructs the part from many sources").

In the 1830s, the Boston Tea Party became fixed in public memory as a celebratory symbol of American nationalism. At that time, political battles raged between the backcountry Jacksonian populists and the more establishment Whigs, whose party more derived from a close identification with the Founding Fathers and a desire to preserve a conservative revolutionary tradition.

But this was more than a hairdresser's version of history.

Issues of slavery and conflicts between Federalism and States' Rights came to the fore. Another central issue during those tumultuous times was the removal of Eastern tribes to the trans-Mississippi West. Greed, corruption, and mismanagement had a catastrophic effect on Indian Removal. The Jacksonians' triumph led to national disgrace. The Cherokees, in particular, suffered extreme trauma, which was preserved in private memory and family traditions. The expression "Trail of Tears," a journalistic invention, was only seared into public memory years after the tragedy.[3] For conservative Cherokees, the event was referred to in their language as "the driveaway," with connotations of animals being led to slaughter. The large death toll combined with the inability to carry out proper burial rites gave the situation a sense of unreality, disbelief, or denial, as well as unmitigated sorrow. Such conditions might in other times have motivated active resistance or given rise to a Ghost Dance, but absolute deprivation made resistance inconceivable. Theologian Jaroslav

Pelikan's idea that "tradition is the living faith of the dead" seems relevant here.

Big Cove, 1957-1960

At this juncture I'd like to take a detour and reconstruct private memories of the Big Cove that I encountered as a young graduate student. I already had completed two years of graduate study at the University of Pennsylvania, where I was immersed in the four-field approach. Exposure to such professors as A. Irving Hallowell, Anthony F. C. Wallace, and Alfred Kidder II afforded me some background on Native North America.

The decision to engage in fieldwork with the Eastern Cherokees was quite fortuitous. I knew a little bit about the Southern Appalachians from visiting my sister while she attended Black Mountain College, that great experiment in America's higher education. Paul Kutsche, one of my classmates at Penn, had also briefly attended Black Mountain, and he had just spent the summer of 1956 doing Cherokee research under the auspices of a three-year project out of the University of North Carolina. Over coffee, I asked him about the prospects of my joining the project. I applied and was conditionally accepted without funding. Fortunately, Penn had a small amount of money for summer fieldwork. I was awarded all of $300 and was on my way.

John Gulick headed the project, but my closest colleagues on the field team were Paul Kutsche and Charles Holzinger and his family. Later, near the close of the project, Bob Thomas was recruited to help shape the final report, *Cherokees at the Crossroads* (1960). We resided in Big Cove in an abandoned Quaker schoolhouse, next to the Pentecostal Holiness Church.

Big Cove was created after the Removal in 1839 as one of the five contiguous kin-based communities that constituted the core of what would become the Qualla Boundary (reservation) of the Eastern Band of Cherokee Indians. While there may be archaeological remains of individual households in Big Cove that predate Removal, there is no clear evidence of a discernable village site. Owing to its topography, Big Cove historically has been considered the most isolated of the five original post-Removal Cherokee townships.

Big Cove has also been regarded as the most culturally conservative segment of the reservation. While other towns had their medicine people and traditionalists, generations of anthropologists flocked to Big Cove. If you laid down all the anthropologists end to end . . . that might be considered a good thing from a Cherokee perspective! Leading the charge was the brilliant and genial James Mooney, to whom all subsequent Cherokee anthropology could be considered a footnote. His successor, Frans Olbrechts, was less well received by his Cherokee hosts and hostesses. Frank Speck, whose knowledge of Eastern Woodland Indians was unsurpassed, was well liked and always referred to respectfully as Dr. Speck. In one brief summer, William H. Gilbert collected much ethnographic material, including valuable data on kinship and social organizations. He also did good service by collating much of the scattered literature on the Eastern Cherokee.

Leonard Broom and one of my mentors, John Witthoft, conducted significant fieldwork prior to the University of North Carolina's project of 1955–1959. I always considered John Witthoft to be a model candidate for what would become the McArthur Genius Award. However, the efforts of these and later anthropologists were only made possible by an impressive lineage of Cherokee intellectual collaborators. Mooney relied heavily on Swimmer (Ayunaii) for myths and medical knowledge; Mooney was also assisted by the venerable John Ax, by Suyeta, Tagwadihi, and Ayusta. James Wofford was his key informant in the Indian Territory. Mooney trained and encouraged a bright young man named Will West Long (Wili Westi). Will developed an encyclopedic knowledge of Cherokee traditions and assisted several later generations of anthropologists. He was eulogized by Witthoft with a three-page obituary in the *American Anthropologist* in 1948. Mollie Sequoyah and two of her sons, Lloyd and Amoneeta, continued the dialogue with outside researchers. I will be forever indebted to Lloyd Sequoyah for most of what I know about Cherokees. He was my patient mentor, my colleague, and travel companion on two trips to Oklahoma.

The aims of the University of North Carolina Cherokee Project were to train some students and to produce a contemporary account of Eastern Cherokee society that would document current issues and prospects and be accessible and, hopefully, useful to Band members. Cherokees had long been critical about the uselessness and potential danger of previous anthropological inquiry. Nevertheless, members of the field team were allowed a great deal of latitude in research topics. The general project design considered culture change and focused on Big Cove as a conservative baseline and Painttown as a more acculturated community. I was originally scheduled to do Rorschach testing in Painttown that could complement data collected by Kutsche, both in Big Cove and in a White Mountain community in Kentucky. However, after collecting about ten protocols I became discouraged and abandoned the psychological testing. I rationalized my decision by telling myself that I was not interested in individual pathology and social anomie, which I didn't have to go to an Indian reservation to study. I refocused my attention on surviving traditions. I became interested in studying those institutions and beliefs that the Cherokees themselves considered to be traditional.

I was influenced by William Fenton's ideas of cultural persistence as opposed to culture change and by his notion of "up-streaming" that involved looking at current beliefs and practices to discover clues to the past. I labeled my variant of this approach "iceberging," meaning that by studying surface features of recognized traditions a deeper and more complex underlying structure might be revealed.

One of the first things I noticed in Big Cove was the persistence of traditional gender roles. There was still a fair amount of farming being practiced, and, except for clearing the fields and helping in the harvest, this was primarily a female domain. Women's work was continuous, regularly paced, whether in working the fields collectively, harvesting fish, managing the household, attending to child rearing, or making crafts. The world of men extended beyond the household and featured hunting, lumbering, trading, and other activities involving high energy expenditure interspersed with slack periods of inactivity. My first paper at the American Anthropological Association meetings in 1957 was on this topic; a much more elaborated version was published years later as "The Petticoat Government of the Cherokees."

I also began working more exclusively with Lloyd on medicine and related matters. At this time, I was less interested in ethnobotany and more concerned with the change, persistence, and accommodation in Cherokee medicine. This became the subject of my 1958 master's thesis and was later published in Bulletin 180 of the Bureau of American Ethnology.

I also had an opportunity to build on the pioneering description of the *gadugi* or free labor companies by Frank Speck and Claude Schaeffer. It became clear to me that these groups were vestiges of the red or military branch of this older hierarchy or dual political organization of Cherokee towns. At least three *gadugi* groups operated in Big Cove in the recent past. They provided an economic and communal safety net for local group members.

A fourth interest ultimately became the basis of my doctoral dissertation on the ballgame, also known as *danahwah usdi* ("little war"). This topic opened up aspects of traditional war ritual and warriorhood. The ballgame was still played as an exhibition for tourists. I was surprised at the amount of ritual still associated with the game. My first intention was to write a short article that would update Mooney's classic account. However, I soon realized that a comprehensive description and analysis would require monograph-length treatment. I entertained thoughts of publishing the dissertation and even prepared several revised drafts. However, I put off completion of this manuscript and never got back to it. I am happy that other scholars (namely the late Marcia Herndon, Tom Vennum, and Michael Zogry) found the dissertation useful in their accounts of the ballgame.

While working on these topics I seemed to be running against the traffic of *Cherokees at the Crossroads*. Acculturation, progress, modernity, community, value orientations, and modal personality structure were the hot topics of the day. My research into the past reeked of old-fashioned, moldy-fig, salvage ethnology. I know I roused the suspicion of many Cherokees as well. Who was this young white guy who was spending so much time with Lloyd Sequoyah and other elders? Was something conspiratorial afoot?

Although Big Cove remained a pocket of conservatism, "the times, they were a'changin'." A few years earlier, community effort, organized along *gadugi* lines, cleared the way for power lines so that electricity reached the farthest corners of Big Cove. This failed to precipitate an immediate revolution. People feared electric bills, and they preferred their old, reliable Roman Eagle wood-burning stoves for cooking and heating. Telephones and televisions awaited the fu-ture—let alone computers, cell phones, and tape recorders. Several Big Cove families embraced the challenge and promise of progress. Seaborn and Sally Bradley ran an award-winning model farm. It was Sally who first introduced me to the delights of sourwood honey.

Wilbur Sequoyah, the school bus driver, lived with his wife in a modern ranch house. But the epitome of the progressive lifestyle was achieved in the large stone-front residence where Georgia and Roy Blankenship raised their remarkable family. I was privileged to rent a room here in 1960 during the final phases of my doctoral research. Later the impressive building was purchased by the tribe for a senior residence. The house has since been razed.

Big Cove in 1957 was still quite impoverished. Yet its residents found ways to survive through self-reliance, communal sharing of resources, small tribal and governmental relief efforts, and through various forms of temporary employment—mostly in the summer. Education was a source of hope for the future. Problems of public health prevailed: high rates of alcoholism, some incidence of tuberculosis, obesity, and the chronic scourge of diabetes. The missing limbs of people like Nanny Driver and Lawyer Calhoun remain fixed in my mind. Conservatives continued to consult native practitioners, while at the same time availing themselves of the services of the agency hospital.

Crime existed at a more or less constant rate but usually occurred under the influence of alcohol. Alcohol entered Big Cove from the stills of local moonshiners and from surreptitious expeditions across its mountains to Cosby, Tennessee. Stories were told about men consuming some of the illegal liquor on the way home, getting drunk, falling asleep, and being mauled by Russian boars. I recently found out that these fearsome creatures with their razor-sharp tusks had been imported around 1900 by a lumber baron who had clear-cut a mountaintop near Murphy for a private menagerie of exotic animals. The boars easily escaped and proliferated in their new environment. Drunken men were frequently "lawed" by their wives for self-protection. A few murders and burglaries occurred each year. I vividly recall one instance when I went to visit Lloyd, who was staying with the Wolf sisters and their 50-year-old mentally-impaired brother, Walker Wolf. As a boy, Walker was said to have been lured into the woods by the Little People and was frightened out of his wits to such an extent that he lost the power of speech. Anyway, I crossed the suspension bridge near the grammar school and Huskey's grocery store and followed the trail northward on the opposite side of the Raven's Fork River. Suddenly, a man jumped out of the weeds and pointed a pistol at my head. I can still see the glint of its shining silver barrel. It was Wade Wolf, who spent most of his adult life in and out of jail. He had just robbed a tourist shop in downtown Cherokee. We were casual acquaintances. He said "Oh, it's just you, Ray" and lowered the gun. "You won't tell anyone where I am, will you?" I lowered my head and replied "No, Wade" and continued on my way to see Lloyd. During my fieldwork I never heard of any drug trade, unlike the situation now.

In the late 1950s I learned the truth of Gregory Bateson's maxim, "the map is not the territory." Big Cove was a large, bounded area intersected by the Raven's Fork River and its tributaries. It contained impressive mountainsides and a limited amount of fertile bottomland. The Big Cove Road entered from the east, off Highway 441 and a short stretch of National Park land. The road followed the course of the river from a roughly north–south direction. In my time, the Big Cove Road was a graveled, tire-flattening passageway that connected the lower Stoney area with upper Big Cove. The road operated as a moccasin telegraph controlling the flow of information back and forth throughout the community. Automobiles were less common in 1957, and people did a lot of walking.

At some levels Big Cove acted as a single community; at other levels it was an amalgam of separate settlements. Big Cove was politically represented by two elected members on the Tribal Council. The community also came together for various competitions at the annual Fall Fair. An early member of our field team, Hester Davis, identified five named sections within Big Cove's boundaries: Upper Big Cove proper; Straight Forks; Bunches Creek; Galimore Creek; and Stoney. Many of these sections had their own Cherokee names.

Four Baptist churches and one Pentecostal church were located in Big Cove. Membership could be quite fluid. Many culturally conservative Cherokees felt no contradiction in following traditional beliefs and practices while still attending church regularly. Often Christianity was espoused only in life crises, like impending death. I went to the funeral of Adam Welch at the head of Galimore Creek. Adam was a staunch traditionalist who spoke little or no English. It was claimed that he chose to join the church on his deathbed, but he expired before he could be properly baptized. At his funeral, the preacher proclaimed that Adam had died a Christian and used as precedent the conversions of the two thieves who confessed their sins while being crucified with Jesus on Calvary Hill.

The separate sections of Big Cove were closely connected by clusters of kin. These sections were spatially linked together by an intricate network of paths. While the Big Witch section of Wolftown was twenty miles away by car, the distance was significantly shorter by foot. Big Cove's borders were more porous than generally assumed. Another mistaken assumption is that Big Cove was a relatively pristine, untouched area. Its solitary splendor, however, was penetrated by a single-gauge railroad spur for logging in the 1920s. Its roadbed along the ridgeline can still be traced today. A lot of lumber was hauled out of Big Cove. The present landscape comprises secondary or tertiary regrowth forest and is maintained on a sustained yield basis.

The secular hub of Big Cove was the grade school, where white Principal Ralph Hatcliffe held forth. Hatcliffe was a strict disciplinarian who was not averse to physical punishment. He was feared by the students but admired by their parents. Students who welcomed spring by enjoying pungent ramps were forced to stand alone and have their mouths washed out with soap. Incidentally, ramps (*Allium tricoccum*) had a wide geographic distribution, even extending to my home base of Chicago. Chicago's name derives from an Algonquian term for ramps. We could have been called Ramptown. Ironically, our present Mayor, Rahm Emanuel, whom I renamed Ramp, is both scant in height and notorious for his foul mouth.

Getting back on course, the Straight Forks area is intermediate between Bunches Creek and Upper Big Cove. A large boulder sits where the river branches off in different directions. According to local tradition, James Mooney once decided that this confluence would be a good fishing spot. Supposedly he asked Will West Long for a ceremony to attract fish. Mooney then stood on the rock with outstretched hands and recited the incantation. When he finished, he leaned back and seven rattlesnakes suddenly appeared, and the panicked Mooney jumped into the river. Later he bawled out Will for giving him the wrong ceremony.

The farthest removed corner of Upper Big Cove was—and remains—a bastion of cultural conservation. Up upon the Raven Rock cliffs overlooking a vast vista, members of the Calhoun family reside. Lawrence and Lawyer Calhoun were repositories of much traditional knowledge, and the revered, recently deceased Walker Calhoun attempted to revive cultural self-awareness among his followers. He drew much of his inspiration from his uncle, Will West Long, who is buried just outside the household. Again we are reminded of Jaroslav Pelikan's view of tradition as "the living faith of its dead."

In retrospect, the Cherokee project of the late 1950s succeeded in fulfilling its goals. A number of students gained field experience, and the tribe was given access to the results of the research. But rather than producing a useful compass indicating where the Eastern

Cherokee had been and where they might be headed, the collected data and interpretations have receded into history. Much interesting material from the project is entombed in the archives of the Wilson Library at the University of North Carolina: fieldnotes, genealogies, census materials, psychological tests, and five valuable project reports by Robert K. Thomas.

A reissue of *Cherokees at the Crossroads* appeared in 1973 with a thoughtful epilogue by Sharlotte Neely (then Williams). Sharlotte points to an improving economic situation, the growth of the tourist industry, decreasing isolation, new housing, improved educational facilities, increasing language loss, an aloofness to pan-Indianism and the Red Power Movement, a concerted attack on archaeologists and their disturbance of graves, a decline in farming, and the disappearance of the *gadugi* organization. Sharlotte also presciently observes that, while the Cherokees have always been adaptive to changing situations, adaptation is not necessarily accompanied by the disappearance of traditional knowledge. As Susanne and Lloyd Rudolph also concluded from their research in India, there can be a modernity of tradition. Indeed, this crossroad choice between modernity and tradition is not a zero-sum game.

It's hard to realize that 40 years have elapsed since Sharlotte's reassessment of *Cherokees at the Crossroads*. Many of the trends she spotted continue unabated, such as the steady growth of tourism and the baby boom. The biggest change, of course, has been the advent of casino gaming. The per capita payment to enrolled members of the Band has lifted many families above the poverty level. Additionally, about 17 percent of the approximately 3,000 full- and part-time casino employees are enrolled members of the Band. Casino profits have been reinvested in tribal infrastructure, in health and educational programs, and in the purchase and preservation of important off-reservation archaeological sites. The most notable acquisition was the ancient mound site of Kituwah, a sacred mother town adjacent to the reservation. Remote sensory devices have revealed the structure and extent of the mound site, but direct excavations have been prohibited. More recently, the historic site of Cowee near Franklin, North Carolina, has also been purchased and is presently being studied for non-intrusive techniques by archaeologist Kathryn Sampeck and her team.

These tribal actions and other developments signal a positive valuation of tradition. The revitalized Museum of the Cherokee Indian, as well as the Sequoyah Birthplace Museum in Vonore, Tennessee; the reconstructed eighteenth-century village; the refocusing of the Outdoor Drama; the continued popularity of the Qualla Arts and Crafts Mutual; the restoration of the historic Vann House; and the increased number of fairs and festivals—all these developments testify to the significance of tradition in maintaining Cherokee identity and strengthening the economy.

Traditional arts, in particular, are enjoying a renaissance: high quality works in carving and sculpture are being produced; traditional stamped pottery, which was once on the brink of extinction, has made a strong comeback; basketry has achieved new standards of excellence; outstanding forms of beadwork, finger weaving, and silversmithing are also enjoying a growing market. The performing arts, including music, dancing, and storytelling, are very much alive and have commercial appeal.

The artistic explosion has important economic consequences in not only invigorating tourism but also in slowing down the rate of mobility and out-migration. The Qualla Boundary, like other reservations, and rural communities more generally, faces a chronic problem in keeping its younger population at home in the absence of a suitable jobs base. Engagement with the gaming industry, employment in tourism, or the opportunity to make a living as artists and crafts people—all help to keep Band members at home.

But what of Big Cove? Its former isolation has been compromised. The Big Cove Road is now paved; camp grounds and public fishing areas abound; housing has been upgraded; up-to-date schools have been built near the entrance to the Stoney area; even the stray dogs are fat. Television, perhaps the main culprit in native language loss, is found in nearly every household. I wonder about the number of cell phones and computers. The cost of this forceful entry into the modern world is a loss of privacy. Except for some of its more remote locales, Big Cove is no longer sheltered from the din of downtown Cherokee.

When I was exposed to the four-field approach to anthropology as a graduate student, we were taught that ethnography—or, more precisely, ethnology—was based on comparison. As a result, students were required to take classes in World Ethnography and a variety of areal courses. Later at the University of Chicago, several faculty sensed that our students were forsaking the comparative approach for a mess of monocultural pottage. Marshall Sahlins and I led the fight to require all students to gain mastery of at least two different cultures or culture areas. Sadly, this requirement faded away in the mists of post-modernism.

Early on, I became interested in comparing what I was learning from North Carolina Cherokees with other groups. Cherokee–Iroquois comparisons had been pursued for a long time, based on known linguistic relations. However, Cherokee culture was deeply embedded in a larger Southeastern pattern that prompted comparisons with the Creeks and other Muskegon peoples. But the most obvious comparison was with the Cherokee Nation in Oklahoma. Here, I was stimulated by conversations with Bob Thomas. I believed the heart of "Cherokeeness" remained in the East. My impression from the literature was that very little authentic Cherokee tradition survived in the West. Bob tried to convince me otherwise and talked about the creative spirit of Cherokee culture and living traditions moving westward. He had written a classic account of the Redbird Smith movement of the so-called Nighthawk Keetoowah faction.

I became excited about venturing to Oklahoma and taking Lloyd Sequoyah along. He might help me gain access to some of the conservative leaders. It would be an educational experience for both of us. I was interested in how he would relate to Oklahoma Cherokees. But mostly I looked forward to Lloyd's company.

I should mention that in the late 1950s, the Eastern and Western Cherokees seemed worlds apart. Few Cherokees had travelled west. In 1951 a delegation from the Cherokee Historical Society went to Oklahoma to bring back the sacred fire that now burns perpetually from a gas jet at the Mountainside Theater. (But more on this later.) Journeys from Oklahoma to North Carolina were both rare and awe-inspiring. These resembled a pilgrimage to the Holy Land. Prophecies abounded in Oklahoma about a permanent return to the paradisiacal homeland. The only local Western Cherokee I knew about was Guy Bark, who had married a Big Cove woman and lived on a remote mountaintop. It wasn't until 1984 that formal diplomatic relations between the Eastern Band and the Cherokee Nation were restored at Red Clay, Tennessee, where the last council meetings were held before Removal.

In August of 1958, Lloyd and I set forth at the crack of dawn on a clear summer day. I remember travelling west through the shimmering Cherokee National Forest. By dusk we reached the outskirts of Corinth in northern Mississippi. We rented a motel room and went for dinner at a nearby roadside cafe. The waiter eyed us suspiciously from a distance and then came over and declared, "We don't serve

Negras." I wish Lloyd had replied, "I don't eat Negras," but I don't want to add these unspoken words to his angry stare.

The next day we arrived in Tahlequah in late afternoon. We stood on a busy corner where Lloyd would stop passers-by and greet them by saying hello (*siyo*) and introduce himself by saying, "I'm a Cherokee from North Carolina, I belong to the *Ani gilo hi* clan." Usually there was no response. One woman curtly answered, "I'm five-eights," and hastened off. Someone suggested that we drive to Stillwell where there was a denser population of Indians.

In Stillwell we added to our plea the old standard line "Take us to your leader." One kind soul took pity on our plight and gave us directions to the nearby residence of George Hummingbird, the then Vice Chief of the United Keetoowah Band. George welcomed us warmly and embraced Lloyd as a brother after learning that they both belonged to the same clan and also shared the same clan on their father's side. We were invited to an impromptu gathering of elders, where over quiet conversation we were served bowls of homemade vegetable soup, bean bread, and scraps of deep-fried fatback.

The next day George and his activist brother Gus gave us a tour of the countryside. That night we were invited to Muskogee to have dinner with George's son, Rabbit, who was a crane operator. After dinner Rabbit asked about some medicinal herbs that were unavailable in Oklahoma. Lloyd recognized the plants and promised to send him some when he returned home. Rabbit then went into the bedroom and returned with a pair of pants, which he handed to Lloyd to seal the deal. Cloth, and before that, animal skins, were recompense for the medicine man and considered instrumental in the efficacy of the treatment. I was duly impressed that this tradition was still alive and well in the heart of the city.

I kept pestering the Hummingbirds about whether it would be possible to visit the Nighthawk people. They weren't very keen on the idea, since as good Baptists they didn't appreciate what they regarded as a return to paganism. Moreover, in their activist efforts to maintain Cherokee treaty rights, the United Keetoowahs found little support from the Nighthawks, who wanted nothing to do with the government. Finally, as proper Cherokee hosts, they consented to take us to Stoke Smith's ceremonial ground outside of Vian. Stokes was Redbird Smith's youngest and only surviving son.

Stokes and the Hummingbirds put aside their differences and chatted amiably. Stokes was soon impressed with Lloyd's knowledge of Cherokee ways. Stokes told us about the dances and the significance of the central fire. He recalled that a few years back some white gentlemen from Cherokee, North Carolina, came and wanted to take some of the fire back to the East. Stokes didn't trust the visitors and thought the request was presumptuous. But to get rid of them he disappeared and returned with some coals that he had lit with his cigarette lighter. This is the fire that eternally burns from a gas jet at Mountainside Theater in Cherokee.

While fire, as the earthly incarnation of the sun, is certainly a central feature of Southeastern ceremonialism, the idea that the sacred fire was transported over the Trail of Tears and never extinguished doesn't fit with what we know about New Fire rituals. Comparative evidence shows that a new fire was kindled to mark a new annual cycle, often at Green Corn ceremonies. Special fires were also built for war parties, ball games, and curing ceremonies.

Among the Creeks at New Tulsa ceremonial ground, where I was an adopted member for over 25 years, in preparation for Green Corn the charred remains of the old fire are carefully removed and deposited on a mound at the edge of the square ceremonial grounds. Fresh, uncontaminated black earth is brought in and shaped into a new circular hearth. Later, four specially selected logs are placed on this hearth and at the appropriate time are ignited with the help of special herbs and kindling. The fire is kept burning and may be fed with deer or beef tongues during the duration of the ceremony, and then the fire is allowed to die out. Such ethnographic detail may be distracting but is necessary to demonstrate how traditions can be over-simplified and distorted in transmission.

Stokes Smith also honored us by bringing out the sacred wampum belts. He draped them over some outdoor metal chairs and allowed us to inspect them. The belts once belonged to the Cherokee Nation and commemorated various treaties. The belts had indeed survived "the trail where they cried." They had become heirlooms of Chief John Ross's family. When the Redbird Smith protest arose in the late 1890s in opposition to the Allotment Act and the dissolution of the Cherokee Nation, the leaders "borrowed" the belts. Through interpretation of the symbols woven into the belts, the belts became the basis for a reconstituted Cherokee religion. These belts have become more and more sacred over time. Today they are rarely displayed in public. Before we left, Stokes tape-recorded a message for the elders of Big Cove, explaining traditional beliefs and offering to bring back the Fire and the new religion, a dream that was only realized decades later through the combined efforts of Bob Thomas and Walker Calhoun.

Our trip was successful. We attended a stomp dance, and Lloyd was convinced that these were not Cherokee dances. While driving through the Cookson Hills early one evening, a deer bounded across the road. Lloyd's eyes lit up. Though he was over sixty years old, he had never seen a deer before. The deer population in the Southern Highlands had been hunted to near extinction. Deerskins were once the major export commodity in the Colonial Period.[4] And the deer was to the Cherokees much as the buffalo was to the nineteenth-century Plains Indians. Presently the deer population has rebounded with a vengeance and poses a public danger as a nuisance and bearer of Lyme disease.

During the whole trip Lloyd was very careful with his money. Occasionally he'd buy a small tin of snuff, but that was about it. Before we left, we went to a craft store and Lloyd splurged on some eagle feathers that were illegally for sale. He later distributed these treasured items to his closest friends. Traditions about the special powers of eagles and memories of the ancient Eagle Dance are still viable.

Let me end with a final postscript on wampum. In the late 1990s, the Cherokee ethnomusicologist Charlotte Heth and I were invited to preview the exciting new cutting-edge laser light exhibits at the Museum of the Cherokee Indian. One exhibit baffled me. It concerned a Cherokee elder who, during pre-Removal days, hung a wampum belt in a Cherokee council house and predicted dire times ahead—but, if the People followed the Cherokee Way, symbolized by the white path of beads down the center of the belt, they would survive as a people. When he completed his talk, the wampum belt suddenly burst into flames. But the fire soon subsided and the wampum belt survived, indicating that the Cherokees, after some difficulty, would also survive if they continued on the White Path.

While the idea of the White Path was familiar to me, I never heard anything about flaming wampum belts. I asked Museum Director Kenny Blankenship about it, and he assured me that the story was well known on the reservation and also in Oklahoma. I told him I had spent a lot of time in Oklahoma and never heard of it.

A few years later, I read an excerpt from a medicine man's expert testimony on the Tellico Dam project, also known as the snail darter case, in which the Little Tennessee River would be dammed and many early historic Cherokee settlement sites and graveyards would be inundated. It was pretty much the same narrative displayed in the museum. However, I was shocked to learn that the testimony was offered by none other than my consultant and fellow traveler, Lloyd Sequoyah. I later found a full version of the text in my dear friend Barbara Duncan's wonderful collection *Living Stories of the Cherokee*. The pieces of the puzzle began to come together. I'm pretty sure Lloyd knew little or nothing about wampum belts before our visit to Stokes's grounds. But where in the world did the inflammable wampum come from? Then I remembered that Lloyd had been an off-and-on member of the Pentecostal Holiness Church, in which a central symbol was a flaming cross. Suddenly it all came together! I learned that living traditions can take some circuitous twists and turns, but this does not make them any less meaningful.

NOTES

1. This paper was originally presented as the Keynote Lecture of the 49th Annual Meeting of the Southern Anthropological Society in 2014. I wish to thank Robbie Ethridge, President of the Society; Lisa Lefler, who performed yeoperson service in organizing the Program and editing these papers; Tom Belt for his kind introduction and help in translations; members of the Eastern Band of Cherokee Indians for their past and present generous hospitality; and finally my loving wife Karen, for making all things possible.

2. According to some accounts, the inspiration for the assembly line came from Ford's tour of a Chicago Stockyard meat-packing plant that he took during a visit to the 1893 World Columbian Exposition. He viewed with interest the disassembly line that involved the use of the Hereford Wheel, a solid wooden wheel about six feet in diameter. Freshly slaughtered steers or pigs were attached to the face of the wheel and rolled through a series of successive stations where skilled workmen systematically dismembered and butchered different parts of the body. In reaction to this cutting-edge technology, Ford supposedly had an "ah ha" experience and envisioned a reverse process whereby the disassembly line became an assembly line.

3. The first use of the phrase "Trail of Tears" seems to have come from a Choctaw chief upon his arrival in Little Rock after the ordeal of Removal. In an 1832 interview with a reporter from the *Arkansas Gazette*, he described the journey as a "trail of tears and death" (Langguth 2010, 164–65). The phrase circulated rapidly in Northern newspapers. The Cherokee *nu no du na tlo hi la* (Rozema 2003, 40) or *nunna dual tsyny* (Perdue and Green 2007, xiv), roughly translated as "the trail where they cried," seems like a secondary, later transcription into Cherokee of an already widely disseminated expression. It is, perhaps, significant that James Mooney never uses the expression "trail of tears" in his monumental *Myths of the Cherokee*. Tom Belt said Cherokees never called it "trail of tears"; instead the Cherokees in Oklahoma used a word for when you drive or push livestock (like a cattle drive or herding)—so it would be translated "when they drove them here" or "when they pushed or herded them here," *tsi du ni hi lo tlv (hlv) i.* Sometimes

a term was used that translated "when they ousted them here." In other words, they didn't come here on their own. Occasionally North Carolina Cherokees used the term that means "when they put them over the top to the other side," meaning put them over the mountains, *tsi du ni wo hi la tv nv i.*

4. The Southeastern deerskin trade of the first half of the eighteenth century is ripe for reanalysis. From the Native side, we need to know more about the ethno-ecology of the deer population; more about the nuanced hunting techniques, including spiritual beliefs and practices; more details about the dressing and tanning of deerskins by women would be welcomed; and more about the transportation of deerskins to the trading post by water and by human porters, many of whom were probably captives or slaves. The interaction with traders whereby exchange value was determined and quantifiable currency established demands closer study. The conflicts between Native ideas of barter as ritualized exchange and market capitalism calls for further exploration. From a Native perspective, manufactured cloth became, in many ways, a symbolic surrogate for deerskins. For a brief period, the deerskin trade became a temporary deterrence to settler colonialism. These dynamics deserve deeper explication and analysis.

On the other side of the Atlantic, the strong demand for deerskins has never been clear to me. Deerskins were valuable (and fashionable) for items of clothing as apparel, as material for furniture upholstery, for bookbinding, and for belts and braided twine. This juncture of Western history witnessed the beginning of the industrial revolution. Perhaps the early machinery was driven by leather belts of Native American origin, soon to be replaced by stronger material (?).

WORKS CITED

Langguth, A. J. 2010. *Driven West: Andrew Jackson and the Trail of Tears to the Civil War.* New York: Simon & Schuster.

Perdue, Theda and Michael D. Green. 2007. *The Cherokee Nation and the Trail of Tears.* New York: Viking.

Rozema, Vicki. 2003. *Voices from the Trail of Tears.* Winston-Salem, NC: J. F. Blair.

Recreating Trickster: Negotiating Cultural Continuity through Discourse

Hartwell S. Francis

Introduction

Meeting with speakers and recording their interactions is critical language preservation and revitalization work. There is a dearth of recorded naturally occurring language interaction for languages of small populations of speakers. Researchers generally work with a single speaker or a few speakers one at a time to elicit language structures for linguistically oriented publications. Learners are often only presented with language structures in lists and other non-communicative formats. Meeting with and recording speakers interacting in their language provides naturally occurring language interactions for research and education. Further, speaker meetings reclaim discourse space for gravely endangered languages. Even when speakers are together, discussion often takes place in English. Speaker meetings with set activities provide sanction for non-English-language interactions.

We are working in the Eastern Band of Cherokee community with the Cherokee Speakers Consortium. We host and participate in meetings that are designed to create space for unfettered use of Cherokee language and to develop language study material. One of our central concerns is the loss of domains for the use of Cherokee language in the community. We are also interested in expanding Cherokee language scholarship in the academy. Our work addresses the question of what is lost without community speakers interacting in their language in all domains of human interaction. We find grave loss of cultural transmission as children attend school in the language of another culture. We find grave loss of cultural transmission even in immersion schools, because Cherokee-medium teachers have not had models of presentation of course content in the Cherokee language.

As we develop language models and Cherokee-medium content presentation models with the speakers in the community, the culture of the community emerges in their discourse interactions. As community speakers participate in co-creating Cherokee-language texts, they reproduce cultural styles that are evident in Cherokee literature. In this study we focus on the co-construction of a chaotic or absurd actor and relate that actor to aspects of the rabbit character in Cherokee folklore. The speakers adopt the persona of the absurd actor as they develop the character through an exchange of humorous scenes of the absurd actor's pitiful interaction with the world. The speakers reinforce their community and at the same time develop negative but fictional examples of incorrect cultural behavior. The fictional absurd actor is ridiculed mercilessly, thereby creating a strong model of negative behavior without recourse to rigid rules proscribing behavior.

Collaboration Exercise Methodology

Stick-figure drawings of characters engaged in different activities were distributed, on cards, to language speakers. The cards are designed to elicit target-language statements and questions about one specific activity at a time. The cards each present a single person engaged in an activity. The cards are designed to provide practice with person prefixes and verb stems, two of the most difficult structures encountered by Cherokee language learners. The Third Person

Singular Imperfective Habitual description of the activity is written on each card in Cherokee, in the English alphabet. Instruction is simple and open-ended: in the target language, discuss the activity pictured on the card.

Manipulating different verb words and manipulating different prefixed pronouns are both very difficult language performance tasks for Cherokee language learners. Verb words are made up of material that indicates tense (location in time), aspect (temporal extent) and mode (speaker perspective on the situation expressed by the verb base). Cherokee language has ten semantic person categories that are referenced by sixty distinct pronouns, each of which has two basic contextually conditioned forms, some of which have further contextually conditioned forms. The person pronouns are prefixed to one of five stem forms to create, in part, Cherokee-language sentences.

The discussion card for the brief conversation under consideration here indicates the activity *cry*. The card shows a rough stick-figure drawing of a person holding her or his head. Tears are falling from the figure's eyes, and tears have pooled below the figure. The card comes from a set of 16 cards. It is labeled 5. The Cherokee Third Person Singular Imperfective Habitual verb word sentence *Atsoyihoi* (she/he cries) is written on the card in the English alphabet.

During this exercise, the speakers and research recorder were ranged around the room, principally around a central conference table. The group met nearly weekly for lunch. After lunch, we held open or themed Cherokee-language discussion and recorded the discussion for research and education. There were twelve participants, including the research recorder. In the interaction based on the *cry* activity card, five participants spoke and the other seven listened. The brief conversation recounted below occurred in the middle of a meeting to go over the set of activity cards.

A Summary of the Conversation

In the interaction selected for presentation here, Speaker One (S1) begins by soliciting participation. S1 is holding the card and with the card engages other members of the group in discussion of the card.

Turn01: S1: *Kag soi?* (Who is next?)

S1 makes an attempt to read the card, but S1 is incompletely successful with the language in this case. S1 has admitted the need for language practice, and the other speakers will often assist one another with the language in their work together.

Speaker Two (S2) does help S1 by reading the card.

Turn02: S2: *"Atsoyiho'i,"* adiha. ("He/She cries," it says.)

S1 then picks up the statement—but moderately modified. S1 also broadens the discussion by teasing S3 and, in a shift from the Habitual of the card to the Present, stating that S3 is crying.

Turn03: S1: Oh, *atso[hi]ho'i*. S3 *atso[hi]ha*.
(Oh, she/he cries. S3 is crying.)

S3 gamely participates, both to continue the discussion and to correct S1. In Turn04, S3 adopts the persona of the character represented on the card. (S3 does not generally cry.) Despite the First Person structure, S3's statement is fictional.

Turn04: S3: *Gatsoyiho'i.* (I cry.)

S2 elaborates on the characterization of S3 that S1 and S3 are developing. S2 provides one of the reasons for the fictional behavior of S3. At the same time, S2 reinforces the re-emerging community standard for language for the Imperfective Habitual form for the activity pictured on the exercise prompt. And again, the statement is not a factual statement about S3.

Turn05: S2: *Nogwu yusvna adela,* **atsoyiho'i.**
(When he runs out of money, he cries.)

S4 with glee confirms the fictional characterization of S3 and reinforces the correct language structure.

Turn06: S4: **Atsoyiho'i!** (He cries!)

S1 rejoins the conversation and further elaborates on the characterization of (fictional) S3 that is developing. S1 continues to use a moderately unsanctioned form. S1's elaboration of S3's character is again fictional.

Turn07: S1: *Nole uditasdi yusvnelvno,* **atso[hi]ho'i.**
(And when he runs out of his drink, he cries.)

S3 picks up and reinforces the ongoing elaboration. S3 reinforces the emerging community standard structure, although in a First Person Singular form.

Turn08: S3: *Sday* **gatsoyiho'i.** (I cry hard.)

S5 expands the context of the fictional S3, in part based on the Imperfective Habitual structure of the target concept. S5 also adopts First Person Singular structure. S5 provides a First Person Singular variant that is the predicted pronunciation (stem glottal fricative alternates to glottal stop in First Person Singular context) in the literature on Cherokee language. By adopting a First Person Singular form, S5 shifts emphasis from S3, opening fictional First Person identification to the group.

Turn09: S5: *Ugitsvda utsvgv. "Yagtsvgv,* **gatsoyi'o'i."**
(The next day he's sick [from drinking]. "When I'm sick, I cry.")

S2 returns to the theme of money and references per capita payments that community members receive from the community corporation. S2 lives about forty miles from the meeting. Unlike S5, S2 completely adopts the developing fictional character. S2 adopts a First Person Singular structure without indication of a direct quote.

Turn10: S2: *Agisgi,* **digatsoyihoi** *yagwagsvnel adela.*
(Even though I get it [per capita payment],
over there I cry when I run out of money.)

S1 elaborates on the theme of per capita payment by indicating that the per capita money is already spent, on credit perhaps, before it arrives. S1 has adopted the repeated emerging standard form for the First Person Singular target structure.

Turn11: S1: *Aya si yigalukvnano, dusvno nogwu* **gatsoyihoi.**
(As for me, and even before it [per capita payment]
comes, it has run out and then I cry.)

S3 picks up and participates in S1's elaboration with a Second Person Singular structure. S3 has accepted S1 as the locus of the developing fictional character.

Turn12: S3: *Halenisgo.*
(You begin [to cry even before money arrives].)

S2 retakes the fictional identity and imagines speaking as the developing fictional character. S2 references community leadership here. The fictional character in this turn becomes an ungrateful complainer. Despite community largesse and profligate personal spending, the fictional character sees others as responsible for lack of funds.

Turn13: S2: *"Na gayohl si," gadisgo, "Gatsv widanihasga adela?"*
gadisgo. ("It's so little," I say. "Where are
they putting the money?" I say.)

S4 picks up the theme of greed and profligacy by speaking as the fictional character. S4 more profoundly adopts the developing fictional character with the emphatic interjection *yo* which is characteristic of impassioned conversation.

Turn14:   S4:   *Yo aniyhgogi! "Dvnehgwo," andisgvgi.*
(They're liars! "It will increase," they said.)

S5 as self observes some validity in the sentiment of the developing fictional character before adopting the persona.

Turn15:   S5:   *Udohyudi. "Kagono atsawanv? Higo iyv*
tsunisdikagwu!" (That's true. "Who is putting it in their pocket? It's such a small amount!")

Turn 15 ends the discussion. Throughout the discussion, with each turn, the speakers and non-speaking participants are following the development of the fictional persona and laughing at each elaboration of the fictional persona.

Discussion

Throughout the participation, the speakers are co-creating their language and culture. At the beginning of this interaction in Turn 1, S1 solicits the support of the group. S1 is holding the card, and in the larger context it is clear to all that it is S1's turn. Because S1 is somewhat insecure in the language and in the exercise, S1 solicits assistance, not by asking for assistance but by indicating (moderate) crisis in the context of the exercise. The manner in which S1 solicits assistance and then the manner in which the group co-construct an imaginary actor provide evidence for the process of replicating Cherokee language and the culture represented by Cherokee folklore.

The Rabbit character of Cherokee folklore, among other characters, gets into trouble by acting outside of accepted norms. Rabbit gets into trouble when Rabbit tries to take on the characteristics of other animals. Because Rabbit transgresses by adopting alien characteristics, Rabbit can be identified as a representative of the trickster complex. In the story of the Rabbit and the Otter, the Rabbit attempts to profit by stealing the Otter's more beautiful coat. In the story of the Rabbit and the Bear, the Rabbit gravely injures herself/himself by attempting to do the things that the Bear can do. Rabbit ends up harming herself/himself as a result of misguided behavior, behavior that runs counter to Rabbit's physical nature. These tales provide examples of negative behavior and the harmful results of negative behavior, without proscribing behavior.

As the speakers develop and adopt the persona of an absurd actor, they are setting cultural norms for behavior without proscribing behavior. In this way, the speakers reproduce a culture based on positive and negative examples that is interested in consensus, cooperation, and individual choice. The absurd actor is childish, unconscious of consequences, ignorant of the needs of others, greedy, and addicted to drugs.

The participating speakers take turns over the course of a short conversation centered on the artificially introduced crying activity. In our work, we often experience the Cherokee cultural ideal of consensus playing out in language work meetings. The speakers are often involved in developing contemporary elementary education curricula vocabulary. In formal meetings, if the speakers do not reach consensus on the Cherokee gloss for a word, they set the word aside for consideration and revisit the word in subsequent meetings. In the conversation presented here, the speakers quickly and organically reach a thematic consensus and participate in elaboration of the theme.

Conclusion

In the Cherokee cultural ideal, human actors are not told how to be-have. No one presumes to proscribe the behavior of another sentient being by setting out rules. Instead, anecdotes about improper behav-ior are shared. Cultural participants laugh at anecdotes of improper behavior, and in this way proper behavior is reinforced and encour-aged. This cultural mode for reinforcing and encouraging proper behavior conflicts with the mainstream cultural mode of setting out rules to reinforce and encourage proper behavior. In the mainstream school system, for example, students are told what not to do—e.g., Don't run in the hallway. The modes for reinforcing and encourag-ing proper behavior clash and cause tension for cross-cultural par-ticipants who have not analyzed either culture.

Negotiating Intersubjectivity as Methodology: Ethnographic Fieldwork and the Co-Production of Knowledge

Brandon D. Lundy, Mark Patterson, and Alex O'Neill

Abstract

How is ethnographic knowledge fashioned and impressions managed during power-laden, discursive interview events? This chapter examines ethnographic encounters with foreign investors, development workers, and government officials in Guinea-Bissau as a way to explore intersubjectivity as a site of meaning making. These encounters take place in negotiated spaces where the dynamics of the encounter are fluid and contextually sensitive. Through an analysis of the co-production of knowledge, social researchers can begin to examine intersubjectivity within the ethnographic interview as both a shared resource and a potential liability for ethnographic interlocutors. This chapter highlights some of the methodological implications of negotiating and evaluating intersubjectivity.

Introduction

Ethnographic fieldwork is an encounter between the researcher(s) and study "subject(s)" as they codify knowledge deemed worthy of documentation (cf. Bellér-Hann, Ildikó, and Sharshenova 2011; Murtha 2013; Pels 2000; Salinas 2013; White 1999). Deciding, both directly and indirectly, what goes on the record and what remains off, is what we refer to here as *intersubjectivity*. Through an examination of this encounter, social scientists can analyze how we produce knowledge within the ethnographic interview (Marteinson 2006). The postmortem deconstruction of these events provides insights into the discursive act at the meta-layer. As a methodological technique, regarding intersubjectivity as a form of impression management that both makes and masks knowledge provides inroads into multiple levels of understanding including the cultural (i.e., Where and why is this encounter taking place?), the individual (i.e., Who are we and what are we doing/making?), and the interactional (i.e., Why are we talking about this, in this way, at this moment?).

The inspiration for this chapter emerged after thinking about the challenges we encountered as researchers during the consent process for a series of interviews and surveys with entrepreneurs throughout the capital city of Bissau in Guinea-Bissau, West Africa, during January 2014. Protective of their busy schedules and cautious in their willingness to disclose operational details about their businesses, each prospective study participant required clear, straightforward assurances of our aims and objectives, an explanation of why we were interested in their businesses, an introduction about where we came from, and vigorous guarantees that we were not affiliated with the state apparatus. Satisfactorily exposing our honest intentions sometimes took upwards of 30 minutes per meeting, while the face-to-face interaction itself was often completed in less than 15 minutes.

Here, we seek to understand how the ongoing process of building rapport seeps into all aspects of the ethnographic encounter and how this might be considered as a factor in the co-production of knowledge between interlocutors. By reviewing interview vignettes, newly exposed meta-data can provide alternative or additional information, making the overall interpretation of the interview and survey data more robust, rigorous, and valid.

This chapter is divided into four parts. First, the theoretical framing is provided to show how ethnographic encounters can be reexamined taking into account the additional layers of intersubjective ethnographic knowledge co-production. Second, five interview vignettes are briefly presented as examples of ethnographic knowledge co-production. Third, these vignettes are referenced to expose and explore some of the backstage negotiations resulting largely from the rapport-building processes begun during the consent process. The chapter concludes by suggesting how intersubjectivity serves as a bridge between the practice of ethnography and the theory of the co-production of knowledge by considering what intersubjectivity as methodology means for anthropological inquiry.

Intersubjectivity and the Co-production of Knowledge

This chapter builds off of previous engagements with intersubjectivity and the co-production of knowledge by scholars such as Michael Jackson (1998; 2002) by considering a single event, the ethnographic interview, as a way to establish a validity construct through the *triangulation of perspectives*. In other words, there are multiple levels of data, meta-data, meaning, and understanding that can be gleaned from a single interview encounter by deconstructing the event as a communicative act between people. As a point of departure, we primarily focus our analysis on Jackson's first notion of intersubjectivity as "'mutually arising'—as relational and variable" (1998, 7). We do this by presenting interactional vignettes, what we are calling here "events," to deconstruct the processes of rapport building, meaning making, meaning masking, and where these overlap and intersect. While equally as salient to discussions of ethnographic intersubjectivity, treatments of affectivity and ethics (Jackson's second point of departure) and "the dialectic of subject and object" as "a reciprocal and analogical relationship . . . between persons and a world of ideas, attributes, and things that are held in common" (1998, 7) must wait for future analyses.

Reflexive, interpretive, phenomenological, and hermeneutic accounts of ethnographic fieldwork have led to the creation of a methodological canon of qualitative investigations that reach beyond traditional empiricism (Bensa 2006; Bensa and Fassin 2002; Borneman 2002, 2011; Denzin 1997, 2001; Denzin and Lincoln 2008; Gable 2010; Gebauer and Wulf 1995; Lassiter 2000, 2001, 2008; Lassiter and Campbell 2010; Meyer and Pels 2003; Pina-Cabral 2009, 2010, 2013; Strohm 2012; Ulin 1992, 2002, 2004, 2007; White 2011; Wulf 2014). These "places of encounters" are recognized as analyzable spaces worthy of investigation in and of themselves. "Each person is at once a subject for himself or herself—a *who*—and an object for others—a *what*. And though individuals speak, act, and work toward belonging to a world of others, they simultaneously strive to experience themselves as world makers" (Jackson 1998, 8, emphasis in the original).

For example, Quetzil E. Castañeda (2005) challenged the fieldworker to "interrogate the complicated entanglements of subjects and objects" (97). He did not decenter ethnographic fieldwork as practice, but instead shone theoretical light on the fieldwork dynamic to "create new understandings, perspectives, and uses" (2005, 98). This chapter begins to unpack the layers of complex meaning that are evoked and invoked during ethnographic encounters by providing a few samples from interview data on Guinea-Bissau and how these events unfolded to elicit shared and valued knowledge.

According to Paul Rabinow (2009, 6), the act of anthropological inquiry remains an area underexplored. We, therefore, reexamine our ethnographic data from foreign investors, entrepreneurs, development workers, and government officials collected in the small state of Guinea-Bissau in West Africa as processual acts of both *knowledge making* and *knowledge masking*. Considering the ethnographic encounter as dialect illuminates potential methodological underpinnings of anthropological inquiry as communicative and power-laden (Gusterson 1997; Nader [1969] 1974; Ortner 2010). What is shared during an interview is observable, fixable, and transportable through the ethnographic act. What remains unspoken and undocumented is a potential for future engagement, a shared recognition of the individual's agency to remain silent, or an unclaimed byproduct of the interaction, purposefully withheld or hegemonically unnoticed.

The theoretical model advanced in this argument, then, is built on sociality, subjectivity, and temporality. Our innate ability and desire to think and act socially both as a form of cultural identity and actual social relationships have been described in the anthropological canon as "ways of being and ways of belonging" played out on a socio-cultural field (Levitt and Glick Schiller 2004, 1008; see also Bourdieu 1977; Leichtman 2013, 41). An unfortunate result of this social inclusion, however, is the possibility of exclusion. Alterity, in the phenomenological tradition, refers to that which contrasts with identity construction allowing for a unique human ability to distinguish between self and not-self, which therefore leads to the imagining of an existence of alternative viewpoints (Fabian 1983; Fanon 2004; Said 1978; Taussig 1993).

Both alterity and empathy have important roles to play in the intersubjective encounter, with both parties judging, exerting influence, and trying to come to an understanding with and over the other. For the philosopher Edmund Husserl, intersubjectivity was about mutuality (not simply an attribution of intentions), bringing interlocutors in line or reaching a shared and potentially accessible lifeworld through empathy (Duranti 2010, 19-21). Therefore, intersubjectivity does not emerge out of interaction but instead is the possibility of realizing such interactions through actual or trace behaviors. According to Alessandro Duranti, "intersubjectivity [is] a fundamental dimension of human experience and human sociability. . . . When properly understood, intersubjectivity can constitute an overall theoretical framework for thinking about the ways in which humans interpret, organize, and reproduce particular forms of social life and social cognition" (2010, 17). Intersubjectivity is about the possibility of reaching understanding, not necessarily completely achieving it.

Intersubjectivity, as defined above, becomes the lens to view ethnographic encounters. But what seems to be missing from Duranti's exposition of Husserl's conception of "We-relationships" (Schutz 1967) is how these engagements account for power. To clarify this point in her own argument, Mara A. Leichtman (2013, 38) drew on Ann Tsing's concept of "friction" that she defined as "the awkward, unequal, unstable, and creative qualities of interconnection across difference" (2005, 4; see also Beuving 2006).

In order to develop an understanding of intersubjectivity as it relates to power relations, we must also consider the root concept, subjectivity. According to Michel Foucault, "It is not the activity of the subject of knowledge that produces a corpus of knowledge, useful or resistant to power, but power-knowledge, the process and struggles that traverse it and of which it is made up, that determines the forms and possible domains of knowledge" (Foucault 1977, 28; see also Foucault 1980). In other words, "the subject is a reflexive human being who, through thinking, constitutes both the objectifying [externalizing] and subjectifying [internalizing] modes of acting, and is constituted by them" (Skinner 2013, 909). Subjectivity links control and dependence (i.e., subjecting oneself to the will of others through consent or force) with self-identity and self-knowledge (Skinner 2013,

918). Exerting this power in the ethnographic encounter can result in shared knowledge and understanding, a type of consensus building between interlocutors, or it can lead to mistrust, apprehension, withholding, and manipulation. In sum, subjectivity is one's ability to hold multiple power-laden perspectives emergent out of experiences and practices that inform one's lifeworld (Heller 1996). Subjectivity is fashioned from a feedback loop between the individual and the social environment. Self–other formation is an ongoing activity that one cannot remove from temporality without setting up a sentimental and anachronistic lament over whether knowledge can be produced at all (Maskens and Blanes 2013; McHugh 1989).

Lastly, encounters occur in time and space. Events change the subject by being inscribed; they are written down, thought and rethought, interpreted and reinterpreted, forgotten and remembered, discussed and ignored, revealed, remodeled, revised, reissued, and replayed. Simultaneity and then simulacra help us engage with that which has taken place—an event that corresponds with a reality. "Intersubjective time has two meanings, however: shared experience in time, and shared temporal frameworks used to make communication intersubjectively significant" (Birth 2008, 4; see also Fabian 1983, 30–31). Intersubjectivity must establish and reestablish temporal frameworks between interlocutors. We do this by co-creating shared and fixable reference points in time and space. These referents become important parts of the ethnographic encounter as it relates to intersubjectivity as a methodology.

In sum, the proposed theoretical framing employs Husserl's "we-relationships" (i.e., sociality), Foucault's "power-knowledge" (i.e., subjectivity), and Fabian's "coevalness" (i.e., temporality) to explain a form of knowledge production and understanding related to the intersubjective ethnographic interview. We triangulate these perspectives to expose how we go about making ethnographic knowledge with layers of meaning about our subjects, our contexts, and ourselves.

Five Ethnographic Vignettes

We present the following five interview excerpts to illustrate inter-subjectivity as it occurs in ethnographic knowledge co-production. These five interview events were selected to demonstrate different aspects of intersubjectivity as discussed in the framing.

These interviews are from a 2014 month-long research trip to Guinea-Bissau in West Africa. The objective of our research project was to survey the economy, with a particular focus on foreign direct investment and entrepreneurship. A total of 153 formal surveys of commercial enterprises and 11 semi-structured interviews with government officials, business leaders, and non-governmental organization management were carried out in January and February. These surveys and interviews took place in ten different business districts within the capital city of Bissau as well as on the coastal island of Bubaque and in the northern town of Sao Domingos along the border with Senegal. The vignettes all come from the interviews in which the negotiated interactions were less formalized and therefore needed more finesse to socially traverse for both the researchers and interviewees.

The first interview to be discussed took place in the United States in February 2014, just after our return from Bissau. It was with the president of a $30-billion private holdings company, which was in the process of trying to establish a partnership with the government of Guinea-Bissau through the country's acting president. The second interview was with the managing director and son of the owner of a large, privately held transnational corporation with 16 companies located in Africa and Spain. They dealt in groceries, construction, food distribution, hospitality and catering, import/exports, maritime logistics, pharmaceuticals, real estate development, and wine and beverages. Their first foray into the Bissau economy was in 2007 with the production and distribution of water, soda, and beer. Within a few short years, they were major private foreign direct investors in multiple arenas of Guinea-Bissau's economy. The third interview was with a port official and director of a community-based NGO in the capital city of Bissau. The fourth interview vignette is from a Lebanese businessperson, the first in Bissau to assist the government with privatization efforts and the liberalization of the economy in the 1980s, more than a decade after independence. The final interview was with a renowned author and businessperson who established the first technology-based firm in the country.

These interviews all took place within a month of each other during a period of political uncertainty in Guinea-Bissau. On April 12, 2012, a military coup d'état occurred, two weeks before the second round of presidential elections between the run-off candidates, former Prime Minister Carlos Gomes Júnior and former President Kumba Ialá. Shortly thereafter, a third-party candidate, Manuel Serifo Nhamadjo, was appointed by the National Transitional Council to serve as the interim president until new elections could take place. President Nhamadjo was still serving as the acting president of Guinea-Bissau at the time of the interviews. These interviews were selected since each interviewee occupied important public and private positions within Guinea-Bissau's political economy. The interview relationships were unique and complex, fashioned out of specific sets of empirical and commercial considerations, existing and newly developing personal and professional relationships, reputational perceptions, time constraints, socio-cultural backgrounds, and environmental factors. These interviews were also selected to represent both foreign and domestic interests. Two were from large, privately-held transnational corporations, one was tied to an

Intergovernmental Organization (IGO) with hopes of operating in Guinea-Bissau, and the other was already doing so. Another was a long-term foreign investor who held Guinean citizenship and began investing in the country as soon as the economy began to liberalize. The other two interviewees were Guinean citizens, one a business-person and the second a government official and representative of a local Nongovernmental Organization (NGO).

Interview 1

On February 18, 2014, we interviewed Jason, the President of Market Holdings,[1] about his company's interests in Guinea-Bissau. He began with a description of their operations: "We've evolved from a think tank to this corporation that serves as a commercial capital manager for [an] IGO that we seek to fund on behalf of, and that is the arm that we utilize to touch the Guinea-Bissaus of the world." Through the initiatives of the IGO, Market Holdings had access to and partial sovereignty in 33 countries, 25 of which were in Africa. They held $30 billion in collateral, employed more than 30 people in four major US cities, and had several international offices.

Jason was careful in his description of the firm's planned operations in Guinea-Bissau:

> So what we are doing is we are [proposing] ascribing a safety fee, $5 per cubic meter, that is to apply for each [shipping] container. We'll take that safety fee, it is maybe $200 for these big groups per container, and that is not cost prohibitive, but we will take that safety fee, accelerate the revenue of that for ten years, and then we will profit share that. We have the ability, because of

---

1 All names of people and organizations provided are pseudonyms to maintain confidentiality.

the financial algorithms we have, and the relationships we have with Zurich and our capital partners, that we can feel comfortable bringing ten years of revenue and sharing that with the country [Guinea-Bissau]. It is not coming from their treasury. The money is not coming from their constituents. It is coming from the shippers of dangers across the world and we are helping them to make the world a safer place. That is how we can bring foreign direct investment into Guinea-Bissau.

Jason commented on Market Holdings operations in Nigeria, Burundi, Guinea Conakry, Mali, and the Congo, describing their business model as "fearless." His use of the word emphasized the perceived risks from operating in certain countries such as Guinea-Bissau where the political context was uncertain.

Simultaneously, Jason worked to relate interpersonally during the interview, for example, by referencing a popular film:

Are you familiar with the BCCI [Bank of Credit and Commerce International] bank scandal of the 1980s? They made a movie about it, the IBBC, *The International* with Clive Owen. They say the ultimate goal in any conflict is not the conflict itself; it is the debt it creates. It is a system of control. The World Bank did it, partially because they do not want to cede that control. Because, once there is debt there, you have that control. So once we have the debt, then we can force the various sanctions, we are not necessarily worried after that because our relationship with Guinea-Bissau is sovereign, or other countries are sovereign, and that will extend beyond a president. So we have an interest in furthering our relationship with Guinea-Bissau.

Jason's comment about *The International* and the World Bank play into the control that he and his company intend to use and keep once they affiliate. This theme of control reappears later in the interview. In a revelatory moment of candor, Jason mentioned corruption and development synthetically: "To get people to listen to us, we have to give them money. That is the bottom line. People, you know, you can say, hey, I have humanitarian instruments, but, if you don't line their pockets up, they are not going to listen to you." He also alluded to the importance of temporality: "And that fear is there. That $5 per square foot, that is too much. But do you know the cost of money in ten years. Present value calculation of the money that we are giving ten years from now. The *present cost of future* money is exorbitant" (emphasis ours). The second interview was with the head of a similar privately held transnational company, although this foreign corporation had already made significant inroads into Guinea-Bissau's economy beginning in 2007, and by 2014, it had significant investments throughout the country.

Interview 2

Raul introduced himself in Portuguese as the son of the owner of Global Partners. Raul was of medium height with dark hair, blue eyes, and grew dark stubble on his face. The young, well-educated businessperson was dressed in a plaid, pressed shirt and dark jeans, and his demeanor was "all business." We approached him for an interview without having first established any prior contact. We proceeded through a security gate before reaching an English-speaking office manager from India.

While the structure was new, we were told that they had been operating in Guinea-Bissau since 2007, although five more businesses had been added since 2012. Raul agreed to give us 30 minutes for our interview. From initial contact until the interview was completed, our attempts to elicit company-specific information regarding their Guinea-Bissau holdings were adeptly managed, as one fieldnote excerpt demonstrates:

> The young businessperson asked if we spoke Spanish, French, or Portuguese but admitted that he spoke "some English." He called the Indian office manager into his office to assist with translation and proceeded to read over the entire consent form on the back of the survey while we explained the purpose of the research project. Raul asked to be "off-the-record" and did not consent to a recording device [although he did give us permission to take notes]; he was hesitant to answer questions without the consent of his father. . . . Raul explained that his father sought out small countries with populations fewer than one million where natural resources were readily available. The building where the interview was taking place employed approximately 100 people of various nationalities, including Indian, Romanian, Portuguese, and Bissau-Guinean. He explained that there were no security issues contrary to belief of worldwide news that focused on the negative aspects in Guinea-Bissau politics; he never felt threatened by the public, although, there was a security gate and attended guardhouse next to the courtyard gate entrance.

Upon completion of this interview, we were conflicted about how "successful" it had been. On the one hand, we were satisfied that we had been granted access to the person in charge of Global Partner's Guinea-Bissau operations. On the other hand, the information that was forthcoming was carefully released with no specific details on business dealings, profits, or ground-level logistics related

to operating a multi-million-dollar private corporation in a politically volatile environment. In other words, there was a great deal
of knowledge-masking regarding sensitive business operations. In
summary, my geographer colleague opined, "I was also surprised
that we were able to see Raul. I figured we would end up making an
appointment to come back. . . . Given how many projects they had
going on, I was pleasantly surprised at how much time he gave us.
. . . [However,] he was quite matter-of-fact in responding to our questions. At times I felt like everything he said could be looked up in
one of the company's annual reports. He only mentioned the projects
that were successful."

Interview 3

Our local research assistant originally set up the third interview,
which was actually two separate interviews. Castigo was a friend and
neighbor. We interviewed Castigo in relation to both his position
in the privatized port of Bissau and his position as the local partner in a community-based NGO working on computer literacy and
the raising and selling of chickens. We met Castigo on our very first
day in Guinea-Bissau, since he picked us up at the airport. We were
eventually introduced to his daughter and wife and had an excellent
working relationship with him throughout our time in the country.
In one fieldnote, we wrote:

> It proved very difficult to determine a day to interview
> Castigo even though we had socialized with him and his
> family several times throughout the month-long stay in
> Bissau. Perhaps it was the uncertainty of revealing infor-
> mation about the port in which he worked or the strange
> pressure that arises when business is mixed with friend-
> ship, but it took an entire month to finally sit down and

conduct the interview. . . . We were strangers who used
this friendly connection to access knowledge that he had
about the port.

The interview was eventually permitted to proceed as long as it
was conducted off-site and confidentially.

To manage intersubjectivity, we formalized the interview by having a clear list of carefully translated and piloted questions. Castigo
became the teacher tasked with instructing us, as outsiders, on the
intricate details of port operations and the day-to-day management
of his NGO.

Interview 4

Gaston was a jovial father figure whom we initially met in one of
his places of business, a school supplies store, while he was changing over his inventory with the help of a French ex-pat friend from
northern Guinea-Bissau. After our initial survey, we asked if he would
be willing to participate in a follow-up interview. He agreed to coffee
the following day.

On January 16, 2014, we met with Gaston across the street from
our hotel at an expensive cafe. He was known by the staff that worked
there; and in the end, they refused to accept my offer to pay, since
Gaston was my senior. He narrated that he was originally from Leba-
non, but he had traveled throughout West Africa, Europe, and had
even spent time in the United States. He had a seemingly thriving
business in the Gambia in the 1980s, which he shut down and now
deeply regretted. At the time of the interview, he didn't seem overly
optimistic about business prospects in Guinea-Bissau and was in the
process of reducing his inventory throughout the capital.

Learning of my colleague's background as a geographer, Gaston
regaled us with a tale of his first experience in the country when he

imported his first container full of stock from Europe and sold it in less than a day. As the first foreign investor in the country, his products were quite novel and in high demand. This potential was the primary reason he had decided to set up his life here. In the meantime, once his business was established in the early 1990s, he was approached by government officials about a map of Guinea-Bissau he had for sale. They entrusted him to go to France and purchase the license for the map so that they could reproduce it domestically. He had much to say about the bipolar nature of the country possibly stemming from its colonial legacy, independence movement, and subsequent political instability.

Gaston, due to his more than 25 years in the country, was able to provide a detailed account and analysis not only of his personal experiences in Guinea-Bissau, but he was also able to look more broadly at how the situation in the country had changed. He was eternally optimistic and simultaneously greatly disappointed in the direction the country was headed.

Interview 5

On January 27, 2014, we sat down with Gomes, the owner of a technology company, GuineTech. We had known each other since 2007, so we spent some time getting reacquainted. We spent almost an hour discussing his business and the current political situation in the country. For example, early in the interview we asked him, "Did the political situation in the country ever affect the business?" His response was quite telling of his frustrations: "Always. Just to give you an example, after 10 years we managed to build this building here. It was inaugurated in January [1998], and in June we had the civil war and most of the building was hit several times. The building was five months old; it was built in January and the war started in June. We really lost everything; we had a lot of computers. They were stolen and part of the building was destroyed." He continued, "You know, this is the only country in West Africa that has no connection to the fiber optics. There is no connection. Senegal has a connection, Gambia has a connection, and even Guinea-Conakry has a connection along with smaller countries like Sierra Leone. There is a lack of guidance with this . . . The government is the biggest obstacle in this country to development." When asked about the future of the country, Gomes said,

> Maybe, in three years I see the country getting out of this trouble. This is somewhat hard to say, but I believe in the country and I hope, there is more hope than belief, but I think we have done so much for ourselves that it is time to start re-thinking our entire lives and look at what we have done. See the mistakes and hopefully they will be able to guide us. Some of these guys that are campaigning now will ruin the country. Some of them deserve our confidence, but most of them do not.

This type of frank dialogue was possible for several reasons. First, we were speaking in English in his private office. Second, he was also an academic. Gomes therefore recognized the value in what we were there trying to do and trusted the research process and assurances of confidentiality. Third, we had an established relationship, which provided him an opportunity to speak candidly about the country's difficulties to someone who in his view was an "outsider."

Layers of Meaning: Several Stories Contained within a Single Event

The methodology advanced in this chapter, outlined above and used to reflect on the five interview vignettes, is not a new approach to social research. Originally advanced by Husserl (1964) as phenomenology and subsequently adopted in anthropology by scholars like Michael Jackson (1998), engaging intersubjectivity continues to serve as a way to reveal alternative data points from the ethnographic interview process. We refer to this as *triangulation of perspectives*, which we believe helps show changes in the social environment that ultimately help us better understand rapport building and the co-production of knowledge(s) within a single shared event. In other words, one interview contains sub-surface information (*à la* Gregory Bateson) that can be exposed through several techniques employed both in real-time at the moment of interface and afterward during analysis and write-up. Some of these techniques shown above include using empathy, negotiated banter, self-disclosure and revelation, collaboration, purposeful or accidental knowledge masking, discourse analysis, and reflexivity, to name just a few. Ethnographers are well situated for this type of research agenda since communication and therefore tension is always present in fieldwork, and since the ethnographer's task is to shine a light on societal, cultural, and institutional norms, patterns, and processes.

In an effort to negotiate the research process and setting, many social scientists are trained to strip away the agency from their research subjects in the name of validity, accuracy, and consistency. Instead, subjective agency should be left intact and celebrated as a way to help enhance the research agenda as an ongoing effort to co-produce knowledge. By both recognizing and acknowledging our multifaceted intersubjectivity during ethnographic pursuits, researchers can consciously and critically work to better appreciate and comprehend the multiple perspectives of our counterparts and ourselves. Researchers need to be reflexive not just about themselves but also about their suppliers of cultural data and how and why it is extractable in particular ways at particular times. Anthropologists must observe, disclose, and attempt to explain what is brought to the encounter and how these social phenomena shape the subsequent co-produced ethnographic narrative.

For example, once people agree to be interviewed, they have a personal stake in the process of knowledge co-production and usually try to answer all the questions (Interviews 1 & 4). Interviews are social encounters. Therefore, people attempt to shape, manipulate, and sometimes undermine these encounters to gain what they think is to their advantage (Interviews 1 & 3). These underlying intentions help shape the interview dynamics and, ultimately, the outcomes. People are also a product of their biology, using rules of inference to aid recall and restructuring past events to remember them in more positive ways as a coping mechanism (Interviews 4 & 5). Influences on the interview process related to our social needs, contextual circumstances, and variable power dynamics tied to our identities lead ethnographers into complex and fluid social fields that must be explored and documented from a plethora of stances. Response effects and other "threats to validity" then become measurable indicators of negotiable identity through the acts of knowledge making and knowledge masking between the interviewee and interviewer (Aunger 2004). Response effects also reflect contextual shifts in the research setting. Therefore, understanding how knowledge is fashioned becomes a critical part of the ethnographic project.

Additionally, deference or acquiescence effects whereby people tell you what they think you want to know (Interviews 1 & 3), third-party-present effects in which social desirability influences responses (Interviews 2, 3, & 4), or the expectancy effect in which the researcher tends to help mold reactions (Interviews 1 & 5) all play a role in the information that is co-produced in an interview. In order to mitigate these "threats" to the validity of a research agenda, the social researcher is trained to employ a number of counteractive techniques such as: aided recall and the use of landmarks to assist with improving memory accuracy; using various forms of triangulation among study participants, investigators, theories, or methods in the hopes of finding convergence among multiple and different sources of information; providing disconfirming evidence; disclosing assumptions through researcher reflexivity; checking and cross-checking accuracy of collected information with other participants; prolonged engagement in the "field"; collaboration with study participants; and the use of thick description to better capture the complexity of the social field.

What is argued in this chapter is that it is more realistic to manage these threats to validity instead of trying to reduce or eliminate them. These threats may in fact become revelatory when employed as techniques to aid in understanding the ethnographic interview process as a way to engage intersubjectivity and reveal layered data. By returning to the interview transcripts and fieldnotes, much more can be revealed about the ethnographic encounter.

With Raul of Global Partners, for example, surprise and the use of third parties was adopted on both sides. The entire five-person research team was brought to Raul's place of business in order to help gain access by emboldening the researchers in their attempt to "study up." Arriving unannounced was used to disrupt the standard power differentials between the manager of a multinational corporation and the investigators. Raul, however, countered by maintaining three levels of access, holding the interview in his office, refusing to allow the interview to be recorded, not providing specific information on the grounds that his father, the owner of Global Partners, would need to okay any specific transactions made "on-the-record," and by bringing in a third party of his own to help translate on his behalf. This example demonstrates how time, power, and sociality build intersubjectivity and help expose interactive data both in terms of what is said and what is not said.

With Castigo of Community Partners, rapport was established by spending a great deal of time with him as well as by gaining initial access through previous contacts and friends. We worked to transform our relationship from collegial to a student–teacher dynamic in which he taught us about the port operations. This set up an effective arena for knowledge co-production.

In the fourth interview with Gaston, shared interests including maps and the English language were relied upon to establish rapport quickly. Empathy as a social phenomenon was clearly present during this interview in which Gaston unburdened himself over life choices that led him to specific business decisions resulting in his current circumstances. His was an informal conversation over coffee where the interview schedule was tabled and we allowed him a space to create his own life history.

Finally, Gomes was approached because of previous relations beginning in 2007. He had been visited during each return trip to Guinea-Bissau by the researcher. Therefore, rapport had already been established, and he was willing to take time to answer questions regarding his business and thoughts about the political situation with candor. The ongoing practice of maintaining expectations and obligations over time and space assisted in open and effective co-knowledge production.

In discussing these study findings, it becomes clear that a single event can be intersubjectively engaged with and subsequently can host multiple readings. This approach contains important methodological potential as an interpretivist and critical approach to the ethnographic interview, one that can show how ethnographic data is both co-produced and, at times, vigorously shielded from view.

Conclusion

As a methodology, we can collect data by observing and analyzing intersubjectivity because we have been trained to do so since birth. It is our need for sociality which allows us to make direct observations and interpretations about others' discourse and behaviors. Through awkward, somewhat undefined power relations, through the process of subjectification and objectification, tension emerges in the ethnographic encounter that exposes intersubjectivity where it was not as visible before. And it is in the moment of encounter that we embark on the creative process of co-knowledge production and knowledge masking, the outcome of which in combination with the intersubjective analysis enhances the validity of the ethnographic enterprise.

WORKS CITED

Aunger, Robert. 2004. *Reflexive Ethnographic Science*. Walnut Creek, CA: AltaMira Press.

Bellér-Hann, Ildikó, and Raushan Sharshenova. 2011. "Crossing Boundaries, Breaking Rules: Continuity and Social Transformation in Trickster Tales from Central Asia." *Oral Tradition* 26 (1): 71–124.

Bensa, Alban. 2006. *La fin de l'exotisme: Essais d'anthropologie critique*. Toulouse, France: Anacharsis Éditions.

Bensa, Alban, and Eric Fassin. 2002. "Les sciences sociales face à l'événement." *Terrain: Revue d'ethnologie de l'Europe* 38: 5–20.

Beuving, J. Joost. 2006. "Lebanese Traders in Cotonou: A Socio-Cultural Analysis of Economic Mobility and Capital Accumulation." *Africa: Journal of the International African Institute* 76 (3): 324–351.

Birth, Kevin. 2008. "The Creation of Coevalness and the Danger of Homochronism." *Journal of the Royal Anthropological Institute* 14 (1): 3–20.

Borneman, John. 2002. "Reconciliation after Ethnic Cleansing: Listening, Retribution, Affiliation." *Public Culture* 14 (2): 281–304.

———. 2011. "Daydreaming, Intimacy, and the Intersubjective Third in Fieldwork Encounters in Syria." *American Ethnologist* 38 (2): 234–248.

Bourdieu, Pierre. 1977. *Outline of a Theory of Practice*. Translated by Richard Nice. Cambridge: Cambridge University Press.

Castañeda, Quetzil E. 2005. "Between Pure and Applied Research: Experimental Ethnography in a Transcultural Tourist Art World." *NAPA Bulletin* 23 (1): 87–118.

Denzin, Norman K. 1997. *Interpretive Ethnography: Ethnographic Practices for the 21ˢᵗ Century*. Thousand Oaks, CA: Sage Publications.

———. 2001. *Interpretive Interactionism*. Applied Social Research Methods Vol. 16. Thousand Oaks, CA: Sage Publications.

Denzin, Norman K., and Yvonna S. Lincoln, eds. 2008. *Collecting and Interpreting Qualitative Materials*. 3rd ed. Thousand Oaks, CA: Sage Publications.

Duranti, Alessandro. 2010. "Husserl, Intersubjectivity and Anthropology." *Anthropological Theory* 10 (1–2): 16–35.

Fabian, Johannes. 1983. *Time and the Other: How Anthropology Makes Its Object*. New York: Columbia University Press.

Fanon, Frantz. 2004. *The Wretched of the Earth*. Translated by Richard Philcox. New York: Grove Press.

Foucault, Michel. 1977. *Discipline and Punish: The Birth of the Prison*. Translated by Alan Sheridan. New York: Vintage Books.

———. 1980. *Power/Knowledge: Selected Interviews and Other Writings 1972-1977*. Edited by Colin Gordon. Translated by Colin Gordon, Leo Marshall, John Mepham, and Kate Soper. New York: Pantheon Books.

Gable, Eric. 2010. "Worldliness in Out of the Way Places." *Cadernos de Estudos Africanos* 19: 75–90.

Gebauer, Gunter, and Cristoph Wulf. 1995. *Mimesis: Culture, Art, Society*. Berkeley: University of California Press.

Gusterson, Hugh. 1997. "Studying Up Revisited." *Political and Legal Anthropology Review* 20 (1): 114–119.

Heller, Kevin Jon. 1996. "Power, Subjectification and Resistance in Foucault." *SubStance* 25 (1): 78–110.

Husserl, Edmund. 1964. *Phenomenology of Internal Time-Consciousness*. Translated by James S. Churchill. Bloomington: Indiana University Press.

Jackson, Michael. 1998. *Minima Ethnographica: Intersubjectivity and the Anthropological Project*. Chicago: University of Chicago Press.

———. 2002. *The Politics of Storytelling: Violence, Transgression, and Intersubjectivity*. Critical Anthropology Vol. 3. Copenhagen, Denmark: Museum Tusculanum Press.

Lassiter, Luke Eric. 2000. "Authoritative Texts, Collaborative Ethnography, and Native American Studies." *The American Indian Quarterly* 24 (4): 601–614.

———. 2001. "From 'Reading Over the Shoulders of Natives' to 'Reading Alongside Natives,' Literally: Toward a Collaborative and Reciprocal Ethnography." *Journal of Anthropological Research* 57 (2): 137–149.

———. 2008. "Moving Past Public Anthropology and Doing Collaborative Research." *NAPA Bulletin* 29 (1): 70–86.

Lassiter, Luke Eric, and Elizabeth Campbell. 2010. "What Will We Have Ethnography Do?" *Qualitative Inquiry* 16 (9): 757–767.

Leichtman, Mara A. 2013. "From the Cross (and Crescent) to the Cedar and Back Again: Transnational Religion and Politics Among Lebanese Christians in Senegal." *Anthropological Quarterly* 86 (1): 35–75.

Levitt, Peggy, and Nina Glick Schiller. 2004. "Conceptualizing Simultaneity: A Transnational Social Field Perspective on Society." *International Migration Review* 38 (3): 1002–1039.

Marteinson, Peter G. 2006. *On the Problem of the Comic: A Philosophical Study on the Origins of Laughter.* Ottawa: Legas Press.

Maskens, Maïté, and Ruy Llera Blanes. 2013. "Don Quixote's Choice: A Manifesto for a Romanticist Anthropology." *HAU: Journal of Ethnographic Theory* 3 (3): 245–81.

McHugh, Patrick. 1989. "Dialectics, Subjectivity and Foucault's Ethos of Modernity." *Boundary 2* 16 (2–3): 91–108.

Meyer, Birgit, and Peter Pels, eds. 2003. *Magic and Modernity: Interfaces of Revelation and Concealment.* Stanford, CA: Stanford University Press.

Murtha, William Gearty. 2013. "The Role of Trickster Humor in Social Evolution." PhD diss. University of North Dakota.

Nader, Laura. (1969) 1974. "Up the Anthropologist—Perspectives Gained from Studying Up." In *Reinventing Anthropology.* edited by Dell Hymes, 284–311. New York: Vintage Books.

Ortner, Sherry B. 2010. "Access: Reflections on Studying up in Hollywood." *Ethnography* 11 (2): 211–233.

Pels, Peter. 2000. "The Trickster's Dilemma: Ethics and the Technologies of the Anthropological Self." In *Audit Cultures: Anthropological Studies in Accountability, Ethics, and the Academy,* edited by Marilyn Strathern, 135–172. New York: Routledge.

Pina-Cabral, João de. 2009. "The All-or-Nothing Syndrome and the Human Condition." *Social Analysis* 53 (2): 163–176.

———. 2010. "The Dynamism of Plurals: An Essay on Equivocal Compatibility." *Social Anthropology* 18 (2): 176–190.

———. 2013 "The Two Faces of Mutuality: Contemporary Themes in Anthropology." *Anthropological Quarterly* 86 (1): 257–275.

Rabinow, Paul. 2009. *Marking Time: On the Anthropology of the Contemporary.* Princeton, NJ: Princeton University Press.

Said, Edward W. 1978. *Orientalism.* New York: Vintage Books.

Salinas, Chema. 2013. "Ambiguous Trickster Liminality: Two Anti-Mytho-logical Ideas." *Review of Communication* 13 (2): 143–159.

Schutz, Alfred. 1967. *The Phenomenology of the Social World.* Evanston, IL: Northwestern University Press.

Skinner, Diane. 2013. "Foucault, Subjectivity and Ethics: Towards a Self-forming Subject." *Organization* 20 (6): 904–923.

Strohm, Kiven. 2012. "When Anthropology Meets Contemporary Art: Notes for a Politics of Collaboration." *Collaborative Anthropologies* 5 (1): 98–124.

Taussig, Michael T. 1993. *Mimesis and Alterity: A Particular History of the Senses.* New York: Routledge.

Tsing, Anna Lowenhaupt. 2005. *Friction: An Ethnography of Global Con-nection.* Princeton, NJ: Princeton University Press.

Ulin, Robert C. 1992. "Beyond Explanation and Understanding: Anthro-pology and Hermeneutics." *Dialectical Anthropology* 17 (3): 253–269.

———. 2002. "Work as Cultural Production: Labour and Self–identity among Southwest French Wine–growers." *Journal of the Royal Anthro-pological Institute* 8 (4): 691–712.

———. 2004. "Globalization and Alternative Localities." *Anthropologica* 46 (2): 153–164.

———. 2007. "Revisiting Cultural Relativism: Old Prospects for a New Cul-tural Critique." *Anthropological Quarterly* 80 (3): 803–820.

White, Bob W. 1999. "Modernity's Trickster: 'Dipping' and 'Throwing' in Congolese Popular Dance Music." *Research in African Literatures* 30 (4): 156–175.

———, ed. 2011. *Music and Globalization: Critical Encounters.* Blooming-ton: Indiana University Press.

Wulf, Christoph. 2014. "Mimesis." In *Handbuch Pädagogische Anthropol-ogie,* edited by Christoph Wulf and Jörg Zirfas, 247–257. Wiesbaden, Germany: Springer.

Reclaiming the Narrative: Creating and Sustaining Culturally Appropriate University Programs for American Indian Students

Trey Adcock

Abstract

Using Kirkness and Barnhardt's (2001) Four R's approach, the paper will demonstrate both successes and challenges in the development and implementation of sustainable programs for recruitment and retention of American Indian students at a Primarily White Institution of higher education. Historically, the University of North Carolina Asheville (UNC Asheville website, n.d.) has had very few continuous and concerted efforts to recruit, retain, and build relationships with the surrounding American Indian community. This can be seen most clearly in the current institutional data, which shows that the American Indian student population makes up only 0.005 percent of the total student community. However, a recently signed Memorandum of Understanding between the institution and the Eastern Band of Cherokee Indians offers hope for the future.

Introduction

In the spring of 2015, UNC Asheville and the Eastern Band of Cherokee Indians (EBCI) signed a Memorandum of Understanding (MOU) that outlines various ways in which the two parties can partner to develop and implement sustainable programs for the recruitment and retention of American Indian students. UNC Asheville Chancellor

Mary K. Grant commented at the signing of the agreement, "This is an important day as we look to make sure we are an institution that is welcoming and supportive in creating a global multicultural community on campus—and it begins right in our own backyard. This is a partnership that we value" (UNC Asheville News Center 2015). Key features of the agreement include the reserving of ten spots each semester for EBCI students meeting the minimum entrance requirements, an out-of-state tuition waiver for EBCI members, the creation of an American Indian Science and Engineering Society chapter, the development of a Cherokee Language program and an American Indian Studies program, among other items. The EBCI, in return, will provide cultural enrichment opportunities on campus and work to develop internships for UNC Asheville students on the Qualla Boundary.

Former Principal Chief Michell Hicks commented at the time, "Our relationship that we have built will continue to grow and get stronger moving forth. We've built a lot of buildings over the years [in Cherokee] . . . but the most important part of infrastructure, from my perspective, is the minds that we develop. I look forward to seeing the intellectual infrastructure that's going to come out of this university." While momentous for both parties, it also marks a transition away from dialogue to action, something that Primarily White Institutions (PWIs) often struggle to do in a meaningful way (Brayboy 2003). In the following sections I will provide context to the agreement and analyze current efforts using Kirkness and Barnhardt's (2001) Four R's approach to student affairs that will highlight some of the ways in which UNC Asheville has worked to follow through with the MOU agreement. In doing so, I will also discuss challenges and offer recommendations for future initiatives.

My Role

Currently, I serve as the faculty mentor for the Native American Student Association and the director of American Indian Outreach for the university, and I am a joint-appointed assistant professor in the Department of Education and Interdisciplinary Studies. As an enrolled member of the Cherokee Nation, the job of recruiting and retaining American Indian students is both a personal and professional endeavor. The opportunity to work with Native students from various tribes is one of the most rewarding experiences of my professional career. As Karen Francis-Begay states, "When our Native American students succeed, we all succeed" (Hibel 2016). Helping students navigate the complex terrain of higher education is challenging as I, myself, often feel isolated and tokenized being the only faculty member enrolled in a federally recognized tribe. Pewewardy (2013) echoes many of my own personal struggles and experiences in the academy as a tribal citizen. Racism, isolation, cultural conflict, and a lack of institutional support are very real issues that I confront every day. However, this work provides an opportunity to subvert the historical pattern of higher learning institutions ignoring and marginalizing native students. Shotton et al. (2013) in the introduction to *Beyond The Asterisk: Understanding Native Students in Higher Education* argue that:

> Native scholars and practitioners have long struggled with the invisibility of Native people within the academy; often excluded from institutional data and reporting, omitted from the curriculum, absent from the research and literature and virtually written out of the higher education story.

I share the story of one institution's attempt, and my role in it, as an inherent exercise of tribal sovereignty and indigenous methodologies. According to Waterman et al. (2013) indigenous systems value observation and personal experience. Thus, by saying "this is my experience," "this is how I understand," "this is my people's understanding," we are enacting our sovereignty (Waterman et al. 2013, 165). Sharing knowledge in this way is a political and spiritual act.

There is another, albeit often unspoken, goal of this work. Helping foster success with Native students in higher education strengthens and reinforces sovereignty efforts by the various tribes and communities the students come from. In this way, success in higher education can serve as a foundation for citizens of Native nations to utilize formal government structures to develop and pursue goals that will benefit and serve the community and its needs (Brayboy et al. 2012).

Braboy et al. (2012, 27) remind us that:

> . . . pursuing higher education folds into a larger agenda of tribal nation building, and vice versa—that nation building cannot be fully or adequately pursued without some agenda of higher education . . . and accounting for globalization and economic notions of nation building, in order for a tribe to be economically and politically successful, it must also be educationally successful.

Cunningham, McSwain, and Keselman (2007, 5) argue too that higher education is one of the main drivers for economic and social development in American Indian communities. The goal of Native nation building, however, is rarely discussed or acknowledged in the broader field of higher education (Braboy et al. 2012) and, more specifically, on UNC Asheville's campus. The story cannot fully be told without understanding the complexity of American Indian students' relationship to and experiences in higher education.

American Indians in Higher Education

American Indian student opportunities for higher education are often influenced and limited by a complex web of factors including socioeconomic status, life experiences, family expectations and responsibilities, culture, tribal education policies and practices, perceptions about the relevance of higher education for living and working in tribal communities, and goals for work and life beyond the degree (Brayboy et al. 2012, 31). These factors contribute to, but do not entirely account for, a culture of "invisibility" of American Indian students and faculty in all facets of higher education. As Fann (2005, 5) argues:

> The near absence of American Indian students on our college campuses deprives the higher education community of indigenous perspectives and contributions to research and teaching, while at the same time depriving American Indian communities of the contributions that a formally educated workforce can make to Native communities' sovereignty, self-determination, health, education, and economic development.

Lowe (2005, 34) too contends that Native American students continue to be underrepresented both in more prestigious private and four-year sectors of higher education while being overrepresented in less prestigious public and two-year sectors.

For more than fifty years there have been gains in enrollment numbers, degrees attained and the number of Native faculty found on university campuses. However, much of the data associated with American Indians in higher education depict a somber story:

- It is reported that Native American students make up 1 percent of the total college student population (Rafa 2016)

- In 2008, 38.3 percent of Native American students completed a bachelor's degree, the lowest rate of all racial and ethnic groups and well below the national average of 57.2 percent (Shotton, Lowe, and Waterman 2013, 7)

- Seventy-seven percent of all Native American and Alaska Native students are likely to attend college and attain no degree or certification (Rafa 2016)

- Four percent of the Indigenous population in the US have a bachelor's degree compared to 27 percent of whites (Brayboy et al. 2012, 51)

- In 2012, only 26 percent of 18- to 24-year-old American Indian/Alaska Natives were enrolled in college, compared to 37 percent of the total population (Brayboy et al. 2012, 54)

- American Indian students are more likely to attend two-year colleges than four-year colleges (Brayboy et al. 2012, 55)

These numbers are staggering, especially if you consider Cunningham, McSwain, and Keselman's (2007, 1) position that access to quality education in general, and higher education in particular, is key to closing the economic and social gap. Essentially, then, the lack of higher educational success further marginalizes American Indian students and thus undermines tribal sovereignty and nation building efforts.

Paralleling the lack of success in higher education for American Indian students is the lack of pre-college readiness that is reported. According to Fann (2005), only 2 percent of college-bound American Indian and Alaska Native high school graduates have a combined SAT score of 1,100 or better compared with 22 percent of all college-bound high school graduates. Part of the issue is the lack of access to college-prep curricula. Brayboy et al. (2012, 35) contend that American Indian students are most likely to be enrolled in general curriculum courses as opposed to college-prep and advanced placement courses and thus are the ethnic group with the lowest percentage of students who graduated with college-ready transcripts. The Center for Native Education (Rafa 2016) also reports that only 26 percent of Native high school graduates have completed a core college preparatory academic track, far less than any other ethnic group.

Compounding the issue is a lack of research on the topic (Lowe 2005). Tachine (2015) reports that, from 1991 to 2011, in two well-known college student affairs association journals, the *Journal of College Student Development* and *Journal of Student Affairs Research and Practice*, only 1.5 percent of titles or abstracts included Native Americans. Shield (2004, 122) further states that:

> The perspectives by Indian researchers and Indigenous Education leaders are unique, innovative, and very valuable, as there is a tremendous lack of Indigenous authored research in education and which is culturally meaningful to Indigenous people.

A significant issue is the lack of Native faculty in higher education, contributing further to the culture of "invisibility" on college and university campuses. In 2014 alone, out of 54,070 doctoral recipients only 109 were American Indian. Currently, Indigenous faculty make up roughly 0.5 percent of the faculty in four-year-degree–granting institutions and 0.7 percent of the faculty in public two-year institutions, whereas white faculty make up roughly 80 percent or more of the faculty across institutional types (Brayboy et al. 2012). This "invisibility" not only deprives the field of research but also of advocates, change agents, and mentors for Native students. Brayboy et al. argue that there are a number of persistent institutional barriers and burdens that marginalize Native faculty and block their advancement in tenure and promotion. The problem is historic, systemic and multi-faceted.

Kirkness and Barnhardt (2001, 1) argue that:

> From an institutional perspective, the problem has been typically defined in terms of low achievement, high attrition, poor retention, weak persistence, etc., thus placing the onus for adjustment on the student. From the perspective of the Indian student, however, the problem is often cast in more human terms, with an emphasis on the need for a higher educational system that *respects* them for who they are, that is *relevant* to their view of the world, that offers *reciprocity* in their relationships with others, and that helps them exercise *responsibility* over their own lives. [italics in the original]

As a PWI, UNC Asheville has struggled with issues of diversity and inclusion in all facets of campus life and organizational structure, particularly with American Indian populations.

The Institution

UNC Asheville is a four-year, coeducational, public liberal arts institution. It is distinctive in that it is the only designated liberal arts institution in the University of North Carolina system. UNC Asheville is primarily undergraduate, with all programs of study leading to the bachelor's degree, with the exceptions of teacher licensure programs and the master's degree in Liberal Arts and Sciences. UNC Asheville is a member of the Council of Public Liberal Arts Colleges, which consists of 29 member organizations that are state-supported liberal arts colleges. UNC Asheville founded—and recently hosted the 30th annual—National Conference on Undergraduate Research where in

2016 over 4,000 students came to present faculty-mentored research. UNC Asheville ranks eighth in the nation among public liberal arts colleges (*U.S. News & World Report's* "2016 Best Colleges," September 2015), and in 2016 *The Princeton Review* ranked the university number one in its listing of "Best Schools for Making an Impact." The university student population is about 3,800 undergraduate students and another 80 students enrolled in the Masters of Liberal Arts program (UNC Asheville Fact Book 2016).

Demographically, UNC Asheville can be classified as a Primarily White Institution, as its white student body population exceeds the 50 percent mark (Brown and Dancy 2010)—around 80 percent to be more exact (UNC Asheville Fact Book 2016). According to its mission statement, the university attempts to engage the diverse surrounding communities with a range of associated centers, partnerships, and initiatives in order to fulfill our public responsibility to address the needs of our community through a continuum of learning. UNC Asheville has developed a commitment to continuing service characterized by an informed, responsible, and creative engagement with the Asheville area, the southern Appalachian region, the state of North Carolina, and a diverse and increasingly connected world (UNC Asheville website, n.d.). However, the diversity of community members in the surrounding area has largely been invisible on campus, particularly the American Indian population. In terms of diversity-related programming, the school maintains an Intercultural Center and Office of Multicultural Student Programs located within the Intercultural Center, which houses spaces for meetings, social events, and programs involving groups such as Alliance, Asheville Students Interested in Asia (ASIA), Black Students Association, Hermanos Orgullosos en Las Americas (HOLA), the Native American Student Association (NASA), and Hillel, among other student-run organizations.

The issue is that, according to statistics compiled by the Office of Institutional Research, minority students comprised only 10.7 percent of incoming freshman in 2012 and 9.5 percent of incoming freshman in 2013. This is out of a total of 603 incoming students. In 2013 minority students only made up 11.9 percent of total enrollment. According to university statistics, the number of American Indian students never reached higher than 0.55 percent over the past five years. For the 2015–2016 academic year, the university reported twenty American Indian students with nine being enrolled EBCI members, two Lumbee students, one non-enrolled Mohawk student, and eight self-identified from various other tribal communities. Despite being situated within a state with the largest American Indian population on the East Coast, the present Native student population makes up less than 0.005 percent of the total campus community. Paralleling these troubling statistics is the fact that only two Native faculty/staff members work on campus out of a total faculty/staff population of around 680. While frustrating, these numbers are not surprising, as, for centuries, mainstream colleges and universities have struggled to accommodate American Indians and create environments suitable for perseverance resulting in degree completion (Guillory and Wolverton 2008, 58). In addition, the university reports that only two out of 37 people from underrepresented populations held jobs in the executive, administrative, or management fields.

Various initiatives have been undertaken to attempt to address the lack of diversity on campus. In the fall of 2008, under the provost's leadership, the Diversity Action Council was formed and charged by the chancellor to turn words into action. Members were chosen specifically because of their direct responsibility for one or more diversity initiatives/programs on campus. As a requirement for graduation, all students must take a Diversity Intensive course. Ideally, culturally responsive practices would be utilized in all courses.

Realistically, teaching philosophies and methods are not adapting at a fast enough pace to meet the needs of the twenty-first century; therefore, the university utilizes the Diversity Intensive courses to partially fulfill their commitment to diversity as a central aspect of a liberal arts education and to offer students the opportunity to examine their own experiences and values alongside those of others. While various programs have been created, reports conducted, and conversations started, I am reminded of Brayboy's (2003, 72) words about the co-opting of diversity terminology by PWIs. He argues:

> Across America, colleges and universities have appropriated the language of diversity as a way of signaling their commitment to faculty and students of color. This article argues that language of diversity and efforts to implement diversity are bound to fail in the absence of an institutional commitment to incorporating strategies for diversity into their research, teaching, and service missions.

The issue, according to Brayboy (2003, 73), is that PWIs often think diversity is something that can be implemented without necessarily changing the underlying structure of the institution and its day-to-day operations. So, while there have been efforts made, there is still a long way to go to move beyond having conversations on diversity to deeply embedding diverse ideas, perspectives, ways of knowing, and voices into the very DNA of UNC Asheville.

The data presented above are particularly troubling, considering the American Indian population statistics in the state. North Carolina has the largest population of American Indians east of the Mississippi River, totaling more than 120,000 according to the latest Census Data (*A New Vision for Native Students* 2014). There are eight federally and state recognized tribes across the state. The total enrollment of American Indians/Alaskan Native students in North Carolina's public schools (K-12) in the 2012–2013 academic year was 20,597, of which 82 percent were enrolled in school districts receiving federal dollars through the Indian Education Act of 1972 (*A New Vision for Native Students* 2014, 5). The closest tribe to the university, by proximity, is the Eastern Band of Cherokee Indians located about an hour's drive west of the campus, with another federally recognized tribe, the Catawba Nation, sitting just across the state border in South Carolina within a three-hour drive.

Despite the large number of American Indian students in the state, as compared to other East Coast states, when I began my position as a visiting assistant professor in 2012, there was only one EBCI student, no Native American student organization of any kind, and no recruitment or retention plan for American Indian students. As is the case with many PWIs, the history and culture of the land's original inhabitants was and remains largely invisible. The signing of the MOU agreement between UNC Asheville and the EBCI has the potential to transform the way in which the institution builds relationships across diverse communities. However, there are and will continue to be challenges moving forward.

How does UNC Asheville, as an institution of higher education, move past the "asterisk" phenomenon that Garland (2013) and others write about to build community engaged partnerships that are sustainable and culturally relevant for the American Indian students on campus? I recognize that there is not any one model that fits all of the diverse and varied experiences of students coming from the over 560 federally recognized tribes and the various state recognized tribes. In trying to answer the above question, I am reminded of the Four R's model: respect, relevance, reciprocity and responsibility (Kirkness and Barnhardt 2001) that has been developed for student affairs and that has implications for all facets of institutional operation (Martin and Thunder 2013). Using the Four R's model, I will now outline some of the programs put into place over the course of the last four academic years and some ways in which the institution can improve and expand efforts to recruit and retain American Indian students.

Respect

Kirkness and Barnhardt (2001, 7) posit that the most compelling problem that Indigenous students face when they go to the university is a lack of respect, not just as individuals but more fundamentally as a people. The authors go on to lay out various ways in which the values, knowledge, and customs of many Indigenous students are not valued at higher education institutions. Brayboy et al. (2012, 42) argue, similarly, that cultural discontinuity or inconsistency between the student's home culture and that of the institution arises as Native students feel a conflict in perspectives and values leading them to question their degree of belonging at such an institution. Shield (2004) and Huffman and Ferguson (2007) contend that no single other factor has been identified more frequently as a contributing factor for poor academic achievement among American Indians than cultural conflict.

One of the ways that UNC Asheville has helped to foster respect is through the support of the Native American Student Association (NASA). For many of the American Indian students on campus, NASA has become a small family where they can build community, trust, and support for one another. Maintaining a student group for Native students is an important way for incoming students to feel included, safe, and respected (Springer, Davidson, and Waterman 2013). Four years ago it was defunct, but through recent efforts, by students and administrators alike, it has grown to be an intellectual and cultural outlet. NASA has been an integral part of organizing, planning, and delivering events such as the A Tribe Called Red concert that brought together over 200 EBCI community members on campus, finger weaving workshops led by EBCI community members, a Violence Against Native Women workshop with Arming Sisters, panels on cultural appropriation, and an American Indian movie night, among other activities. Through these events the campus community has been able to learn from and with the Indigenous students on campus. Broadening these efforts from NASA into all facets of the campus curriculum is essential to foster the type of respect Kirkness and Barnhardt (2001, 8) envision. Increasing the university's domain of human knowledge to include and respect First Nations cultural values and traditions is a formidable task, but it is a task that we must begin if we are to make the institution more "user friendly" for First Nations students.

Culturally Relevant

The second R in the Four R's model is cultural relevance, which builds off the initial pillar of respect. Kirkness and Barnhardt (2001, 9) argue that:

> If universities are to respect the cultural integrity of First Nations students and communities, they must adopt a posture that goes beyond the usual generation and conveyance of literate knowledge, to include the institutional legitimation of indigenous knowledge and skills . . .

One way to do this is through the promotion of culturally relevant pedagogies and programming. Burke (2007, 2) contends that evidence of Eurocentric, privileged cultural values and traditions are embedded in the homogeneous perspectives depicted in college curricula, which may deny American Indian/Alaska Native students cultural relevance or opportunities for academic success.

This is particularly true at UNC Asheville, where one of the primary cornerstones of the curriculum is a humanities program that every student is required to take. There are four courses designed to span the entire undergraduate experience for students. The courses are titled: HUM 124: The Ancient World; HUM 214: Community and Selves from 300-1700; HUM 324: The Modern World; and HUM 414: The Individual in the Contemporary World. While I will not get into the academic minutia of the titles and governing disciplines, I will say that fairly quickly after I arrived on campus it became clear that the courses either did not include, discounted, or undermined the history, values, and knowledge of Native peoples. However, the institution has recognized the shortcoming of the HUM curriculum and has mandated a re-envisioning of each of the courses to be more inclusive in the perspectives the courses centralize.

Questions of cultural relevancy have helped to guide the development of programming around recruitment and retention for American Indian students on campus. There is a general belief amongst educators and academics that culturally relevant programs can improve contemporary American Indian students' chances for academic success. Martin (2005, 79) posits that cultural relevancy has implications for curriculum, instruction (teaching methods adapted to students' learning styles), evaluation (not limited to standardized tests), and governance. For examples of culturally relevant programming, in all facets of American Indian education, one can look to Tribal Colleges and Universities. At UNC Asheville we have tried to do this through the creation of a Native American Speaker and Performance series. Guests included Paul Chaat Smith (Comanche) of the National Museum of the American Indian, Former Principal Chief of the Cherokee Nation Chad Smith, Perry Horse (Kiowa), the Warriors of AniKituwah (EBCI), Former Principal Chief of the Eastern Band of Cherokee Indians Michell Hicks, annual EBCI stickball games, and a panel on Native health covering topics such as histori-cal trauma, food sovereignty, child social services, and the new EBCI hospital. These events are free and open to the public and meant to build a bridge between the academy and community. Martin and Thunder (2013, 43) contend that these types of culture-based pro-grams help to provide authentic, contemporary representations of Native people, which benefit all parts of the campus community and allow the campus Native community and local Native community a chance to renew bonds.

These events, however, are stand-alone and many students do not attend. The challenge for the institution is to move towards a more inclusive curriculum throughout students'—Native or non-Native—entire undergraduate experience so that learning about, from, and with Indigenous people is deeply engrained into their consciousness. An attempt is currently underway to develop an American Indian and Indigenous Minor program on campus. Martin (2005) argues that the establishment of American Indian studies programs can lead to higher persistence rates for Native students, particularly in mainstream institutions. Cultural relevancy, however, does not sin-gularly mean traditional curriculum. For a curriculum to be truly relevant to the needs and realities of Native students it also must be embedded into policies, rights, and the unique status of Indigenous peoples so that they can fully aid tribal communities and nations in the process of nation building (Brayboy et al. 2012). Many Ameri-can Indian students matriculating through colleges and universities, however, know little about Native rights, policy, or the status of Na-tive communities in the United States (Champagne 2003). For UNC Asheville, this means properly funding the program, hiring Native faculty to develop and lead courses, and retaining Native students to populate the courses. Admittedly, there are political and ideological issues associated with Native American studies programs across the country (Warrior 2008). However, it is my belief that through a curriculum grounded in the political, social, and cultural realities of our students the university can move closer towards embedding cultural relevancy in all facets of recruitment and retention.

Reciprocity

The third R that Kirkness and Barnhardt (2001, 12) describe is reciprocity. Providing examples of relevancy in practice, the authors theorize that, when teaching and learning is a two-way street, "Faculty members and students in such a reciprocal relationship are in a position to create a new kind of education, to formulate new paradigms or explanatory frameworks that help us establish a greater equilibrium and congruence between the literate view of the world and the reality we encounter when we step outside the walls of the 'Ivory Tower.'" An aspect of reciprocity is for the university to go to the community instead of expecting the community to come to them. One way in which UNC Asheville has tried to foster this type of relationship is through the development and implementation of a course taught at the local high school by a professor in the New Media program. For three semesters this professor has offered an introductory computer and media programming class to high school juniors and seniors on the Qualla Boundary. This has allowed them to gain valuable engagement with college-level courses and begin developing faculty relationships prior to entering higher education. As a result, many of the incoming EBCI students at UNC Asheville have originated from this course and once arriving on campus already have a faculty advocate.

Despite this success, the institution still has work to do in the area of reciprocity. The example above is one instance of the university having a presence and a commitment *in* the community, but the efforts cannot end there. Events such as parent night, counselor appreciation, community meet-and-greets, and UNC Asheville Admissions information sessions that are collaborative in nature and are hosted *within* the community expand notions of reciprocity, demonstrating that the institution is willing to work for and learn *with* the community. Too often, however, the administrative response is "can't they just come to campus?"—reinforcing the belief that the university is an out-of-touch ivory tower.

Responsibility

In terms of responsibility, Kirkness and Barnhardt (2001, 12) suggest that gaining access to the university means more than gaining an education—it also means gaining access to power and authority, and an opportunity to exercise control over the affairs of everyday life, affairs that are usually taken for granted by most non-Native people. I believe one way to do this is through the Family Engagement Model (FEM). Guillory and Wolverton (2008, 61) argue that this intervention-based model can enhance an American Indian student's sense of belonging and consequently leads to higher retention rates among American Indians. This mode, however, not only has implications for recruitment and retention but also for preparing American Indian students who graduate from UNC Asheville to go back into their community with skills and knowledge to serve. According to Guillory and Wolverton (2008) giving back to their tribal communities was the second most frequently cited persistence factor in a study on Native American student persistence.

FEM calls for an expanded approach that includes families in almost every aspect of a student's college experience. The essence of the FEM is to create a family-like environment for Native American students by making family and tribal members an integral component of the educational process of these students (Brayboy et al. 2012). UNC Asheville has begun to consider practices such as an

American Indian alumni luncheon that brings together graduates and current students to discuss issues of curriculum, on-campus jobs, programming, and mentorship. Another idea is to create an American Indian family weekend once a year that seeks to bridge the gap between campus and home life. As Martin (2005, 84) posits, organizing family events on campus once or twice per academic year may assist in maintaining the family ties that are so important to the success of American Indian students. This approach seeks to build on student and family strengths and, thus, invite the community into the college or university's activities. Brayboy et al. (2012) argue that the role of parents in cultivating early expectations for college is critical and is one of the most important factors of retention. FEM as an intentional strategy inherently moves the campus into a culturally responsive model that values community inclusion by seeking consultation and collaboration with families in designing outreach activities. One way I have called for the university to enact FEM is through the creation of a community council of alumni, parents, and tribal leaders to help assist in the planning, implementation, and decision-making process for outreach activities.

Another possible implication of a FEM model and a way to centralize the idea of responsibility, I argue, is through the fostering of student engagement with their home community during and after graduation. Karen Francis-Begay (Hibel 2016) posits that one of the three critical points of information of which key leaders on campus need to be aware is that tribes want a return on their investment. They invest hundreds and thousands of dollars in scholarships for their students to pursue a postsecondary education. The hope for many tribal leaders is that these students return to their community to serve. I have seen this firsthand with the American Indian students I have worked with. One of the initial indicators of success at UNC Asheville has been the students' personal desire to take the knowledge and skills they are acquiring and return to their home community. Some of the current students have discussed wanting to serve their community by working in the school systems, hospitals, in counseling, and various other ways. Students that have this intention tend to be more resilient and more focused and to excel in their course work. UNC Asheville has a unique opportunity to foster this type of learning through the Undergraduate Research Program. In 1978 the National Council of Undergraduate Research was founded on the campus of UNC Asheville and has blossomed into a national organization of individual and institutional members representing over 900 colleges and universities (Council on Undergraduate Research 2016). The central goal of the Council is to provide research opportunities for undergraduates, mentored by faculty members. As Francis-Begay (Hibel, 2016) argues, increasing the number of Native students in research and encouraging them to publish on issues that impact Native people and communities is one way to improve the visibility of Native students and issues in higher education. This past March, one of our American Indian students developed and presented on issues pertaining to tribal sovereignty. Tribal leaders and various members of his community showed up to the presentation to offer support, bridging the gap between the academy and community.

Conclusion

Over the past four years UNC Asheville has experienced success with the recruitment and retention of American Indian students as the population of students has risen from zero to twelve EBCI members—along with the momentous signing of the MOU. In moving forward, there are and will be challenges such as administrative support, funding, staffing, and possibly other unforeseen barriers. However, by using Kirkness and Barnhardt's (2001) work to guide the institution's activities, involving family in all aspects of the students' experience and centralizing the tribal communities, there is hope. It is through these efforts that, as Austin (2005) contends, a university that works hard at recruiting and retaining American Indian students, with the tribal community centrally involved, can enjoy a large American Indian enrollment along with favorable retention and graduation rates for those students. This type of success can be personally empowering and contribute to the broader goal of nation building that tribes seek and, finally, move past the "asterisk" phenomenon at UNC Asheville.

WORKS CITED

A New Vision for Native Students. State Advisory Council on Indian Education Report to the North Carolina State Board of Education. Raleigh, NC: Department of Public Instruction, 2014.

Austin, Raymond D. 2005. "Perspectives of American Indian Nation Parents and Leaders." *New Directions for Student Services* 2005 (109): 41–48.

Brayboy, Bryan McKinley Jones. 2003. "The Implementation of Diversity in Predominately White Colleges and Universities." *Journal of Black Studies* 34 (1): 72–86.

Brayboy, Bryan McKinley Jones, Amy J. Fann, Angelina E. Castagno, and Jessica A. Solyom. 2012. Postsecondary Education for American Indian and Alaska Natives: Higher Education for Nation Building and Self-Determination. ASHE Higher Education Report, vol. 37, no. 5. San Francisco: Jossey-Bass.

Brown, M. Christopher II and T. Elon Dancy II. "Predominantly White Institutions." In *Encyclopedia of African American Education*, edited by Kofi Lomotey, 523–526. Thousand Oaks, CA: SAGE Publications, 2010.

Burk, Nanci M. 2007. "Conceptualizing American Indian/Alaska Native College Students' Classroom Experiences: Negotiating Cultural Identity between Faculty and Students." *Journal of American Indian Education* 46 (2): 1–18

Champagne, Duane. 2003. "Education for Nation-Building." *Cultural Survival Quarterly* 27 (4): 35.

Council on Undergraduate Research. 2016. "About the Council on Undergraduate Research," accessed May 30, 2016, *http://www.cur.org/about_cur/.*

Cunningham, Alisa F., Courtney McSwain, and Yuliya Keselman. 2007. *The Path of Many Journeys: The Benefits of Higher Education for Native People and Communities.* A report by the Institute for Higher Education Policy, in collaboration with the American Indian Higher Education Consortium and the American Indian College Fund. Accessed March 2007, *http://www.ihep.org/research/publications/path-many-journeys-benefits-higher-education-native-people-and-communities.*

Fann, Amy J. "Forgotten Students: American Indian High School Student Narratives on College Access." PhD diss., University of California, Los Angeles, 2005. ProQuest (AAT 3208343).

Garland, John L. "Foreword." In *Beyond the Asterisk: Understanding Native Students in Higher Education,* edited by Heather J. Shotton, Shelly C. Lowe, and Stephanie J. Waterman, xv–xvi. Sterling, VA: Stylus Publishing, 2013.

Guillory, Raphael M., and Mimi Wolverton. 2008. "It's About Family: Native American Student Persistence in Higher Education. *The Journal of Higher Education* 79 (1): 58–87.

Hibel, Andrew. 2016. "Native American Students in Higher Education—The Past, Present and Future" Higher Ed Careers Interview by Karen Francis-Begay, accessed May 19, 2016, *http://www.higheredjobs.com/higheredcareers/interviews.cfm?ID=470.*

Huffman, Terry, and Ron Ferguson. 2007. "Evaluation of the College Experience Among American Indian Upperclassmen." *Great Plains Research* 17 (1): 61–71.

Kirkness, Verna J. and Ray Barnhardt. "First Nations and Higher Education: The Four R's—Respect, Relevance, Reciprocity, Responsibility." In *Knowledge Across Cultures: A Contribution to Dialogue Among Civilizations,* edited by Ruth Hayoe and Julia Pan. Hong Kong: Comparative Education Research Centre, The University of Hong Kong, 2001.

Lowe, Shelly C. 2005. "This Is Who I Am: Experiences of Native American Students." *New Directions for Student Services* 2005 (109): 33–40.

Martin, Robert G. 2005. "Serving American Indian Students in Tribal Colleges: Lessons for Mainstream Colleges." *New Directions for Student Services* 2005 (109): 79–86.

Martin, Steven C. and Adrienne L. Thunder. "Incorporating Native Culture Into Student Affairs." In *Beyond the Asterisk: Understanding Native Students in Higher Education,* edited by Heather J. Shotton, Shelly C. Lowe, and Stephanie J. Waterman, 39–52. Sterling, VA: Stylus Publishing, 2013.

Pewewardy, Cornel. "Fancy War Dancing on Academe's Glass Ceiling." In *Beyond the Asterisk: Understanding Native Students in Higher Education,* edited by Heather J. Shotton, Shelly C. Lowe, and Stephanie J. Waterman, 139–150. Sterling, VA: Stylus Publishing, 2013.

Rafa, Alyssa. 2016. *State and Federal Policy: Native American Youth.* Denver, CO: Education Commission of the States. *http://www.ecs.org/wp-content/uploads/State_and_Federal_Policy_for_Native_American_Youth.pdf.*

Shield, Rosemary White. 2004. "The Retention of Indigenous Students in Higher Education: Historical Issues, Federal Policy, and Indigenous Resilience." *Journal of College Student Retention* 6 (1): 111–127.

Shotton, Heather J., Shelly C. Lowe, and Stephanie J. Waterman. "Introduction." In *Beyond the Asterisk: Understanding Native Students in Higher Education,* edited by Heather J. Shotton, Shelly C. Lowe, and Stephanie J. Waterman, 1–24. Sterling, VA: Stylus Publishing, 2013.

Springer, Molly, Charlotte E. Davidson, and Stephanie J. Waterman. "Academic and Student Affairs Partnerships." In *Beyond the Asterisk: Understanding Native Students in Higher Education,* edited by Heather J. Shotton, Shelly C. Lowe, and Stephanie J. Waterman, 109–124. Sterling, VA: Stylus Publishing, 2013.

Tachine, Amanda R. "Native Americans in Higher Education Are More Than Just an Asterisk," *Huffington Post,* February 22, 2015. *http://www.huffpost.com/entry/native-americans-in-highe_b_6372786.*

University of North Carolina Asheville (website). n.d. "Asheville's University." Accessed May 20, 2016, *http://www.unca.edu/about.*

University of North Carolina Asheville. Institutional Research, Effectiveness and Planning (website). n.d. "Fact Book." Accessed May 20, 2016. *http://irep.unca.edu/fact-book.*

University of North Carolina Asheville News Center. "UNC Asheville and Eastern Band of Cherokee Indians Sign Agreement," May 1, 2015. Accessed May 20, 2016, *http://news.unca.edu/articles/unc-asheville-and-eastern-band-cherokee-indians-sign-agreement.*

Warrior, Robert. 2008. "Organizing Native American and Indigenous Studies." *Publications of the Modern Language Association of America* 123 (5): 1683–1691.

Waterman, Stephanie J., Heather J. Shotton, Shelly C. Lowe, and Donna Brown. "Conclusion." In *Beyond the Asterisk: Understanding Native Students in Higher Education,* edited by Heather J. Shotton, Shelly C. Lowe, and Stephanie J. Waterman, 165–174. Sterling, VA: Stylus Publishing, 2013.

Cherokee Concepts about Health and Healing

James Sarbaugh

Abstract

Health and well-being are maintained in traditional Cherokee communities by carefully balancing the social, and sacred, relationships between all spiritually significant beings, human or otherwise. An imbalance in these relationships results in ill health that affects the entire community. Balance is maintained or restored through ritual practice in which both women and men may play critical roles as trained specialists who rely on medicines, physical therapies, and ritual language and non-verbal means to communicate sacred knowledge. Practitioners must also constantly monitor, evaluate, and make use of new knowledge gained from the surrounding environment, employing methods that are intrinsically conservative, yet dynamic and flexible.

Beginning with the information collected by the missionary Daniel Butrick in the 1820s and '30s, and continuing to the present day, we have written accounts of Cherokee native medicine that make it perhaps the best reported institution of its kind in Native North America. Since the 1880s, scholars such as Mooney, Olbrechts, Swanton, Speck, Witthoft, Thomas, Fogelson, Kupferer, Jack, Anna, and Alan Kilpatrick, Walker, Heth, Herndon, and more recently Lefler, and Altman and Belt, have all contributed original information and insight to this literature. Many of these studies derive in good part from a unique database—scores of documents written by Cherokees in their own language using the Sequoyah syllabary, which was adopted and widely used before Removal in the 1830s. Raymond Fogelson declared that one of these, the *Swimmer Manuscript*—collected, translated, and analyzed by James Mooney and Frans Olbrechts between 1888 and 1932—"is probably the best study of ethnomedicine available for any North American Indian Society" (1975, 115).

The great majority of Cherokee medical manuscripts, or doctor books, consist of what Mooney called "sacred formulas," "prayers," or "songs." According to Cherokee tradition, these songs were the gift of the powerful, man-eating ogre, Stonecoat, who was captured and burned alive by a community of Cherokees. As he was consumed by flame, he "sang forth the entire culture of the Cherokees" (Gilbert 1943, 207). He "told them the medicine for all kinds of sickness . . . and sang the hunting songs for calling up the bear and the deer and all the animals" (Mooney 1900, 320). As understood by Will West Long and told to Frank Speck and Leonard Broom in the 1940s, this was the origin of all the songs known to Cherokees "since before the time of Christ." These songs could aid the people in all aspects of their lives and included vocal music governing dances, hunting, horticulture, medicine, and all social relationships from lovemaking to protection against opponents and enemies. Hundreds of these songs, written in syllabary, have been collected.

As Raymond Fogelson observed, however, "Despite the richness and specificity of all this material, the picture of Cherokee medicine that emerges is highly particularistic and fragmented into discrete bits and pieces. Despite notable efforts by Mooney, Olbrechts, and others to discern a general pattern in Cherokee medicine, there is little overall integration or sense of system in the data" (Fogelson 1974; Fogelson subsequently contributed important information and analysis on Cherokee world view, Cherokee categories of diseases, and the roles and procedures of practitioners of native medicine [1961, 1974, 1975, 1980]).

The great majority of literature on Cherokee medicine has focused attention on the programmatic details of curing and its counterpart, conjuring. Whether intended by authors or not, this has often resulted in portraying Cherokee medicine as based on arcane principles and mysterious practices that may appear outlandish, lurid, and even threatening. Not only has this drawn attention away from a "sense of system" of Cherokee medicine, but as Willard Walker noted (1981, 96), it has tended to draw "attention away from such potentially significant phenomena as the relationships of curers to patients, conjurors to victims, and curers to conjurors. More importantly . . . it has drawn attention away from the curing–conjuring complex as a social institution and its implications for relationships between different communities within a given 'tribe,' between communities of different 'tribes,' and between the 'real people' and such Euro-American institutions as the Public Health Service Indian Hospitals, the public schools, the Bureau of Indian Affairs, and various law enforcement agencies."

One thing that does emerge from this literature, confirmed by the testimony of modern Cherokees in both North Carolina and Oklahoma, is that core beliefs and practices concerning health and healing have persisted in Cherokee communities over time and distance. I'll try to pull together threads from interviews with Cherokees, observations in the field, and published and unpublished archival sources to discuss some of these core beliefs and understandings, particularly as they relate to the social aspects of Cherokee medicine. Hopefully, this discussion will connect, at least loosely, with the contributions in this field that Lefler, Altman and Belt, Holland and others are making today. (Since my own fieldwork was conducted forty years ago, it might be more accurate to say that all my sources are archival.)

There is no better place to begin this discussion than with the story of the origins of disease and medicine that James Mooney collected in the 1880s. He tells that,

> In the old days—in the time when four-legged animals, birds, fish, insects and plants could all talk—they lived with human beings in "peace and friendship." But people increased in number so rapidly that they spread over the entire earth, and animals were cramped for room. Worse, humans developed weapons—hooks, knives, spears, blowguns, and bows and arrows with which they "slaughtered the larger animals for their flesh or their skin." Smaller creatures, such as frogs and worms, they tread upon without regard.
>
> So the animals called a great council to determine how better to protect their common safety. Each animal clan, from bears to grubworms, decided to inflict a particular disease on people to punish them for bad behavior, and to reduce their numbers.
>
> And this was the origin of disease.
>
> When the plants learned that animals planned to bring diseases to humans, they called their own council. They had no great quarrel with people, and determined to help them. "Each tree, shrub, and Herb, even down to the Grasses and Mosses, agreed to furnish a cure for some one of the diseases" that the animals would inflict. "When the doctor is in doubt what treatment to apply for the relief of a patient, the spirit of the plant suggests to him the proper remedy."
>
> And this was the origin of medicine.
>
> (paraphrased from Mooney 1891, 319–22; 1900, 435–36)

Illness, being the result of the breakdown of respectful relation-ships between spiritual beings in the world, is, at root, social in na-ture. As Robert K. Thomas, a Cherokee anthropologist, put it: "A crucial part of the Cherokee world view . . . is seeing the universe as having a definite order, as a system which has balance and recipro-cal obligations between its parts. The individual Cherokee is a part of this system, and membership entails certain obligations. When the Cherokee does not fulfill his obligations, the system gets out of balance and the Cherokee [indicating the collective population] no longer have the 'good life'" (1961, 163; see also Hudson 1976, 317–25).

Al Logan Slagle, a Keetoowah Cherokee, confirms Thomas: "[M]any Indian people share the belief that . . . [h]ealth is the condi-tion of individuals and communities which live and grow in a har-monious, stable relationship with their environment as it continu-ously changes. Health is a kind of freedom and . . . 'wholeness' that can only be enjoyed through discipline" (Lincoln and Slagle [1987] 1997, 268).

Anthropologist Heidi Altman and scholar Thomas Belt, a native Cherokee speaker, provide additional perspective. They describe the Cherokee concept of well-being as predicated on maintaining the world in its natural state, described as *tohi,* which is "fluid, peace-ful, and easy like water flowing," and maintaining the individual in a "centered balanced and neutral state," denoted by the term *osi.* Actions that disrupt these natural states may bring on "illness or other consequences" that can inflict damage on individuals or the community. Healing can only occur by restoring "the world and the individual to the proper state" (Altman and Belt 2009, 22).

Cherokees associate these concepts with the "white path," which Lloyd Sequoyah, a ritual practitioner from the Eastern Band of Cherokee Indians, explained in 1978 as representing "*Duyukta,* the path of harmony, or being in balance . . . the traditional way of the

Cherokee people" (Duncan 1998, 26–27). Traditionally, the "white path" was often graphically depicted on wampum belts with a central stripe of white beads. Among many Christian Cherokees this path is often referred to as the "narrow way to heaven," which is sometimes equated with the clear, white, central margin between verses in the Bible (Fink 1978, 136). Keeping to this pathway is what non-Christian Cherokees mean when they say "peace" or keeping to their "laws" and what Christian Cherokees often refer to as "love" or "righteous path" (Fink 1978, 136; Mooney 1900, 487; Wahrhaftig 1978, 439; Wahrhaftig and Lukens-Wahrhaftig 1977, 231).

Keeping to the White Path will ensure health and harmony. Straying from it, even inadvertently, will result in disease and dissension and all sorts of misfortune. Following the White Path, however, is not a matter of simply keeping to "specific customs or ways of doing things." Rather, it is "a condition of human relationships" that are reciprocal with all living beings. Maintaining these relationships is a dynamic process involving the perpetual pursuit of knowledge and constant monitoring of the environment in order to preserve the well-being of the community (Wahrhaftig 1978, 440; see Jordan 1975, 121-124)

So, like illness, maintaining and restoring health are, at root, understood as social processes. As described by anthropologist Albert Wahrhaftig, most Cherokee ritual can be understood as a means of maintaining or reestablishing respectful, reciprocal relationships that "sacredly strengthen all life in the universe" (Wahrhaftig 1978, 440; see also Wahrhaftig and Lukens-Wahrhaftig 1977, 231-32). These concepts of health and illness could be described as holistic, encompassing the entire solar system, since the sun and the moon are also sentient beings in Cherokee tradition.

In the eighteenth century, health and balance were maintained in each Cherokee town by a headman, assistants, and a seven-man council made up of representatives from each of the seven matrilineal clans. Among other functions, this council oversaw the performance of six major annual ceremonies that were meant to protect the health and well-being of the community. Each clan gathered and, led by its clan councilor, purged using the "black drink," cleansed by going to water, and drank a prophylactic infusion of medicinal herbs to maintain them in good health. And there is some evidence that, at least in some cases, the seven-man council acted corporately in performing healing rites for those afflicted with illness. These practices could be described in contemporary terms as community-based public medicine with a strong emphasis on health maintenance and disease prevention.

Following the Civil War, most Cherokee communities in North Carolina and Indian Territory had established Protestant churches. By the 1870s, when the Cherokee Nation in Indian Territory was threatened by being absorbed into a new national territory or state, Cherokees attempted to re-invigorate traditional community institutions and practices. The organization that initiated this movement adopted what many Cherokees believe was the name given to them by the Creator, calling themselves Keetoowah. By the early 1900s, they had succeeded in establishing reconstituted ceremonial centers, or Sacred Fires, in about half of the communities in the Nation. Each Fire, or Stomp Ground, had officers and a seven-man medicine council with representatives from each of the seven clans. Four times a year they presided over ceremonies that involved purging, going to water, and drinking prophylactic medicine prepared from seven medicinal herbs and distributed to each clan (Lanman 1849, 95; Thomas 1953, 1961).

Janet Jordan, who did fieldwork in the 1970s with Oklahoma Cherokees, was told that the seven-man medicine councils not only had responsibility for fending off and curing illness but for ensuring ample crops, ending droughts, mediating disputes within the community, and negotiating with organizations from outside the community, including county, state, and federal officials (Jordan 1975, 114-119). The core of this revitalized institution, which Keetoowahs described as "religious," might also be described as a community-based public health organization.

Revitalization of native religion and institutions is not the only mode of adaptation that Cherokees have made to protect the vitality of their communities. By the 1960s, most members of Cherokee speaking communities in Oklahoma and North Carolina belonged to a Protestant church. This is unusual among American Indian ethnic groups (Berkhofer 1976). And, while a good deal is still unknown about how widespread conversion was achieved, a key element in this process is that Cherokees, like converts from many other ethnic groups, did not simply adopt Christian ideas and values, they adapted them to their own longstanding principles and tenets (Fogelson 1961, 220; Jordan 1974; 1975, 306-12; Thomas 1953, 88-92).

Raymond Fogelson (1961, 220) has noted that the faith healing tradition was one element of southern Protestantism that helped build a rapport between Native and Christian practice. One Christian convert from the 1820s, Thomas Nutsawi, offers early evidence of this. He had been an "assistant priest" in his community when, at about the age of fifty, he showed deep interest in learning about Christianity. After moving his home near to an American Board mission station, Nutsawi found he had contracted a life-threatening lung ailment. He was cured after he initiated a new form of medical treatment that combined traditional fasting and herbal medicine with Christian prayers "to that savior, who was able, he had heard, to cure diseases."

By 1850, Baptist and Methodist churches, where members could vote many of their own rules, began to accept Native doctors if they were judged sincere in their Christian belief. When James Mooney did his fieldwork in North Carolina in the late 1880s, he found that at least two highly respected Cherokee curers, Inoli and Gahuni, were also Methodist preachers (Mooney 1891, 313-316). Among Oklahoma Cherokees in the early 1950s, Robert Thomas found that "many staunch Baptists," including some ministers, were also Native doctors who saw "no conflict in preaching Christianity and praying to the Thunder to cure disease" (Thomas 1953, 92; see also Kilpatrick and Kilpatrick 1967, 5). Several years later, Raymond Fogelson found similar practices in North Carolina Cherokee communities. As one Cherokee curer explained: "When I conjure, I go by the word of God. . . . If it wasn't in the power of the Creator, you couldn't make anything move" (Fogelson 1961, 220; see also Jordan 1975, 298-301, 309). Jack Kilpatrick described a related blending of traditions. In 1963 in Oklahoma, a "Cherokee woman suffering from chronic headaches was brought on a cot to the Beaver Church campground for a 'Christian' healing service. A medicine man sat at her head while a minister stood at her right and the worshipers collected around her. While the minister silently prayed for his charge, the medicine man arose and lead the group in a stirring rendition of 'Amazing Grace'" (A. Kilpatrick 1997, 132). By the mid-twentieth century, many, if not most, Cherokees considered Christian hymns in their language to be traditional sacred songs. In at least some communities, hymns had been incorporated into more traditional Cherokee ritual practices.

Janet Jordan described one instance of the complex ways in which Cherokee churches, and the social networks they support, have been agents of cultural conservatism, adaptation, and innovation. During her fieldwork in an Oklahoma Cherokee community in the 1970s, Jordan learned that the local fire had been the primary religious organization there until the middle of the 1950s. Drought had struck in 1951 and continued for three years. "The medicine of the medicine council was not working. Medicine men were curing people on their own rather than through the auspices of the entire medicine council." When all seven medicine men on the council worked together, they had "pretty good Cherokee doctors. They used to doctor about anything," according to the former speaker of the medicine council. The head of another, still active, medicine council agreed: "[M]edicine men doctoring individually is what weakened the Sacred Fire organization, 'That was the old Indian way.'"

The preacher at the local Baptist church, although called a "white man" by community members, was a Cherokee of mixed ancestry and respected for his command of the Cherokee language and his knowledge of herbal medicine. He also believed in the type of medicine practiced at the stomp ground [Fire] "if you have faith."

The chairman, or speaker of the medicine council became convinced that "duyu:kta, or the 'truth,' lay on the side of Christ rather than on beliefs of the Fire." He converted and joined the local Baptist Church in 1957. Jordan was told that this resulted in "a 'switching over' from the Sacred Fire organization to the Cherokee Baptist Church." By 1972, the church had formed a new, seven-member nominating committee that included the church deacon, formerly the head of the local medicine council. He described the members as "seven spirits," the term he had earlier used for the seven members of the medicine council. Of the seven, three were women. Two of these were also church officers, and the third was one of the few members of the church who were literate in Cherokee. Although Jordan doesn't say so, it seems likely that the seven members represented each of the clans. The new nominating committee took on the traditional role of the former medicine council, assuming "the responsibility for the well-being of the entire community," which included public and private curing ceremonies involving the laying on of hands, prayer, and hymn singing. Traditional gendered roles that applied to the ceremonial ground were altered to accommodate gendered roles appropriate to a new, more socially viable institution: "[T]he community had incorporated Cherokee meaning into the Baptist faith and adapted it to community needs" (Jordan 1975, 230-232, 298, 306–12; see also 1974, [9]).

Jordan, however, notes that this "switching over" to the Baptist church that she recorded was "no reflection of a case of progressive assimilation, because in at least twenty-six cases the Baptist church preceded the Sacred Fire in the community" [in the late 1800s]. "A process of incorporative integration" was going on at the time, but Jordan predicted, "if the fit between white forms and native meaning becomes too strained, it is the white forms that are likely to be discarded" (1975, 355).

Even if Euro-American forms are retained, native institutions may be revitalized, as happened when the Sacred Fire was rekindled in North Carolina in 1989. The last ceremonial ground in North Carolina went out of use sometime around 1880. When Bob Thomas was doing fieldwork there in the late 1950s, Eastern Cherokees showed interest in rekindling the fire, but plans didn't get off the ground until thirty years later. With Thomas as facilitator, in September of 1989 the head medicine man and most of the officers of the Redbird Smith Fire in Oklahoma, along with some strong song leaders and shell shakers, all drove to North Carolina in six cars to help lay the new fire. Thomas looked at this as an opportunity for "cultural exchange between Oklahoma and North Carolina." The North Carolina people would be learning about the Cherokee Law as restored by the Keetoowahs a hundred years before; and the Oklahoma people would be learning about the Green Corn Ceremony that was lost to them "during Removal times" but still known in North Carolina. The fire lighting and the first all-night dance were a great success, despite a steady down-pouring rain. The North

Carolina Cherokees, whose morale had been low, felt "new hope" (Thomas 1990).

The next year, a four-day Green Corn Dance was planned for August, and Thomas was asked to help organize it. He worked with the most knowledgeable ritual practitioners in Big Cove, and they arranged a four-day event with traditional and innovative elements. One of the innovations was holding a sweat bath "as a purification in place of the 'going to water' ritual and as a replacement for 'taking medicine,' the purgative Black Drink." The Green Corn Dance was well attended, and Thomas hoped that the new fire would have a "big impact" as "an institution not pre-empted by outsiders."

Cherokee healers continue traditions of working together to maintain the well-being of their communities. They rely on traditional knowledge but also constantly monitor, evaluate, and make use of new knowledge gained from the surrounding environment. Their practices are intrinsically conservative yet dynamic and flexible, complex, and sometimes innovative—restoring traditional institutions and creating new ones—qualities that have contributed to the Cherokees' long history of successful cultural adaptation. Their therapies are calculated to not simply cure the physical symptoms of patients but to re-socialize them, reintegrate them into the local community, and restore proper relationships within the community and with the world at large (see Walker 1981, 98). They know that by keeping to "the path of Harmony, of being in balance" they will survive as a people. *Duyukta*. (Duncan 1998, 26-27).

WORKS CITED

Altman, Heidi M., and Thomas N. Belt. 2009. "Tohi: The Cherokee concept of Well-Being." In, *Under the Rattlesnake: Cherokee Health and Resiliency*, edited by Lisa J. Lefler, 9–22. Tuscaloosa: University of Alabama Press.

Berkhofer, Robert F. Jr. 1976. *Salvation and the Savage: An Analysis of Protestant Missions and American Indian Response, 1787–1872*. New York: Atheneum.

Duncan, Barbara R., comp. and ed. 1998. *Living Stories of the Cherokees*. Chapel Hill: University of North Carolina Press.

Fink, Kenneth Ernest. 1978. "A Cherokee Notion of Development." PhD diss., Union Graduate School. UMI Dissertation Services.

Fogelson, Raymond D. 1961. "Change, Persistence, and Accommodation in Cherokee Medico-Magical Beliefs." In *Symposium on Cherokee and Iroquois Culture*, edited by William N. Fenton and John Gulick. Smithsonian Institution Bureau of American Ethnology Bulletin 180. Washington, DC: Government Printing Office.

———. 1974. Medical Anthropology as Anthropology. Paper presented at the meeting of the American Anthropological Association, Mexico City, November 1974. Unpublished manuscript.

———. 1975. "An Analysis of Cherokee Sorcery and Witchcraft." In *Four Centuries of Southern Indians*, edited by Charles M. Hudson. Athens: University of Georgia Press.

———. 1980. "The Conjuror in Eastern Cherokee Society." *Journal of Cherokee Studies* 5 (2): 60–87.

Gilbert, William H. Jr. 1943. *The Eastern Cherokees*. Smithsonian Institution Bureau of American Ethnology Bulletin 133. Anthropological Papers, no. 23. Washington, DC: Government Printing Office.

Hudson, Charles M. 1976. *The Southeastern Indians*. Knoxville: University of Tennessee Press.

Jordan, Janet E. 1974. "Reflections on the Social Aspects of Illness in a Western Cherokee Community." Paper presented at the Southern Anthropological Society meetings, Blacksburg, VA, April 4–6, 1974. Unpublished.

———. 1975. "Politics and Religion in a Western Cherokee Community: A Century of Struggle in a White Man's World." PhD diss., University of Connecticut. UMI Dissertation Services.

Kilpatrick, Alan. 1997. *The Night has a Naked Soul: Witchcraft and Sorcery among the Western Cherokee.* Syracuse, NY: Syracuse University Press.

———. 1967a. "Muskogean Charm Songs Among the Oklahoma Cherokees." *Smithsonian Contributions to Anthropology* v. 2, no. 3. Washington, DC: Smithsonian Institution Press.

———. 1967b. *Run Toward the Nightland: Magic of the Oklahoma Cherokees.* Dallas, TX: Southern Methodist University Press.

Lincoln, Kenneth, and Al Logan Slagle. (1987) 1997. The Good Red Road: Passages into Native North America. Reprint, Lincoln: University of Nebraska Press.

Mooney, James. 1891. *Sacred Formulas of the Cherokees.* Seventh Annual Report of the Bureau of Ethnology to the Secretary of the Smithsonian Institution (1885–86), 301–397. Washington, DC: Government Printing Office.

———. 1900. *Myths of the Cherokees.* Nineteenth Annual Report of the Bureau of Ethnology to the Secretary of the Smithsonian Institution (1897–98). Washington, DC: Government Printing Office.

Mooney, James, and Frans M. Olbrechts. 1932. *The Swimmer Manuscript: Cherokee Sacred Formulas and Medical Prescriptions.* Smithsonian Institution Bureau of American Ethnology Bulletin 99. Washington, DC: Government Printing Office.

Payne, John Howard. n.d. [ca. 1835–39]. Papers of John Howard Payne Concerning the Cherokee Indians. Ayer Collection MS.689, Newberry Library, Chicago. Microfilm.

———. 2010. *The Payne-Butrick Papers,* edited by William L. Anderson, Jane L. Brown, and Anne F. Rogers. 2 vols. Lincoln: University of Nebraska Press.

Thomas, Robert K. 1953. "The Origin and Development of the Redbird Smith Movement." Master's thesis, University of Arizona. Unpublished.

———. 1961. "The Redbird Smith Movement." In *Symposium on Cherokee and Iroquois Culture,* edited by William N. Fenton and John Gulick. Smithsonian Institution, Bureau of American Ethnology Bulletin 180. Washington DC: Government Printing Office.

———. 1990. "Lighting the Cherokee Fire." *Americans Before Columbus* 18 (1): 3,5.

Wahrhaftig, Albert. 1978. "Making Do with the Dark Meat: A Report on the Cherokee Indians in Oklahoma." In *American Indian Economic Development,* edited by Samuel L. Stanley, 409–510. The Hague: Mouton Publishers.

Wahrhaftig, Albert, and Jane Lukens-Wahrhaftig. 1977. "The Thrice Powerless: Cherokee Indians in Oklahoma." In *The Anthropology of Power: Ethnographic Studies from Asia, Oceania, and the New World,* edited by Raymond D. Fogelson and Richard N. Adams. San Francisco: Academic.

Walker, Willard. 1981. "Cherokee Curing and Conjuring, Identity and the Southeastern Co-tradition." In *Persistent Peoples, Cultural Enclaves in Perspective,* edited by George Castile and Gilbert Kushner. Tucson: University of Arizona Press.

Traditional Knowledge and Health: Lessons from the Eastern Band of Cherokee Indians

Lisa J. Lefler

The Cherokee people, or more appropriately, the people of Kituwah, have lived in the Southern Appalachian region for more than 12,000 years. They have lived in one of the most biologically diverse ecosystems in the world, and have done so long enough to have observed, trial-tested, and inventoried thousands of flora and fauna, cosmological movements, climatological changes, and geological phenomena to fill a multitude of volumes.

Some challenge the notion that the "Traditional Knowledge" (TK) of Indigenous people could be considered "science." Western civilizations and their European explorers and conquerors from initial Contact justified the decimation of Indigenous people and their epistemologies by universally condemning them all as savages, primitives, and heathens, thereby devaluing and denouncing them even as human beings. Then as now, Indigenous people were debased and discriminated against yet exploited for their resources, from ginseng to oil, gas, and uranium. In today's world, they are also often exploited for their knowledge and ceremony, and their culture is appropriated for others' monetary gain.

American history is based on the premise that Europeans *discovered* the inhabitants of the Western Hemisphere, implying that the colonizers were the main actors of power who determined what was of importance and that the mere existence of these people of the New

World was trivial until their "discovery" (See, for instance, Bray 1993 and Greenblatt 1993). On the other hand, we were not taught that the millions of Indigenous people populating this hemisphere were *encountered*, with sophisticated societies, languages, cosmologies, cosmographies, and resources. We were not taught that their ways of knowing and living were rich in diversity, wisdom, and *science.* "Science" according to Webster's definition is "knowledge about or study of the natural world based on facts learned through experiments and observation."

By the time Europeans had descended upon them, Native people had highly developed agrarian methods and seed hybridization techniques that provided them a wide variety of cultivated food sources. Hundreds of species of corn, beans, and squash, among many other plants, had been skillfully propagated and diffused. Simply put, Indigenous people had knowledge of genetics (Fedoroff 2003).

Their botanical knowledge rivaled—if not surpassed—that of Western or European science at that time. However, with the genocide that ensued at Contact (about 1500 AD) much of the population who held that knowledge were annihilated. Eastern Band of Cherokee Indians enrolled member Kevin Welch, founder and former director of the Center for Cherokee Plants, explains:

> As a people, we Cherokee have forgotten a large amount of our woodland knowledge, perhaps as much as 85–90 percent of our traditional uses for wild plants. The mountains of Southern Appalachia have a huge biodiversity and Cherokee people have had several thousand years to learn to use this resource. At one time, it would have been commonly known when, where and what plants and animals might be found during certain times of the year. Having this knowledge of available resources

makes the difference between just living and living well!
(Veteto et al. 2011)

The idea that the first inhabitants of the Western Hemisphere were unintelligent, primitive, and/or "savage" has been one of the biggest lies of Western education and religion. Only in recent decades have texts been introduced to Western academies that contradict these notions by providing evidence to the contrary—as if evidence were necessary.

We know that Indigenous knowledge has perpetuated an understanding of how we, as organic entities, are related or connected to all other natural things. And through the discovery of modern physicists Western science affirms that this is a valid paradigm—yet does not recognize the contributions of TK as an originator of that paradigm.

Native scholar Vine Deloria wrote:

> Our task is to discern from the continuous introduction of new elements of knowledge and experience a coherent interpretation of the scheme of things. Traditionally, Western people have called an inquiry of this kind *metaphysics*, and its task has been to discover the structure and meaning of what was real. The word itself has become somewhat frightening to Western peoples because of their inclination to make metaphysical conclusions an absolute canon of faith, thus imposing abstract principles on their practical understandings of the world around them. (1979, 11)

TK is knowledge that is anchored in the natural and spirit worlds. This of course has brought great pause to Western scientists. Dawn Martin-Hill (2008, 8), a First Nations scholar, writes of TK and power, understood as the historic struggle between science and religion:

> The cultural diversity of Indigenous peoples is addressed through the recognition that Indigenous knowledge is attached to the language, landscapes, and cultures from which it emerges.

It moves beyond the Western hierarchical system of knowledge and moves beyond mere attachment to the land. She refers to Indigenous scholars Battiste and Henderson's explanation that "Indigenous peoples regard all products of the human mind and heart as interrelated with Indigenous knowledge. They assert that all knowledge flows from the same source: the relationships between a global flux that needs to be renewed; the people's kinship with other creatures who share the land, and the people's kinship with the spirit world."

Martin-Hill summarizes that "the validity of Indigenous knowledge is noted in Indigenous universal natural *law*, which posits that knowledge is spiritually based and ecologically derived" (10). Native peoples have known for millennia that we are all made up of the same "stuff." We are not only *in* nature, but part *of* nature.

My lack of understanding as an academic was challenged by my understanding as an Appalachian person who had spent much time with my mother outside, in nature. She would often remark that we are part of a magnificent and wondrous place if we only took the time to be a part of it and understand it. Because of this experience, in my fieldwork I was more apt to listen—during both casual conversations and ceremony—to elders who spoke about our relationship with the world around us. My problem was making it fit with my ego of intellectualism, into which I have invested tremendous resources and energy as a graduate student and professor. Friend and Cherokee elder Tom Belt reminded me that we are part *of* this place, not just *from* this place.

My intent is not to overgeneralize, but the hallmark of Western thinking is to reduce elements and concepts to their smallest parts—to compartmentalize thinking. Indigenous thought allows for how things work in unison for the big picture—holistic thinking. In order for us, as Western-trained thinkers, to broaden our understanding of the TK principle that all things are connected, we can best understand through Indigenous language and practices. Vine Deloria knew this well. He begins, in his seminal work, *Metaphysics of Modern Existence* (1979, vii): "The fundamental factor that keeps Indians and non-Indians from communicating is that they are speaking about two entirely different perceptions of the world."

His elaboration of this is fundamental to how we come to know Native science, or TK, and how it can make for realistic application in our work as healthcare providers and environmental conservators—two fields that for many in the Western academy and practice are seen as distantly related at best. Deloria explains:

> Growing up on a reservation makes one acutely aware of the mysteries of the universe. Medicine men practicing their ancient ceremonies perform feats that amaze and puzzle the rational mind. The sense of contentment enjoyed by older Indians in the face of a lifetime's experience of betrayal, humiliation, and paternalism stuns the astute observer. It often appears that Indians are immune to the values which foreign institutions have forced them to confront. Their minds remain fixed on other realities.

He continues,

> In a White man's world, knowledge is a matter of memorizing theories, dates, lists of kings and presidents, the table of chemical elements, and many other things not encountered in the course of a day's work. Knowledge

seems to be divorced from experience. Even religion is a process of memorizing creeds, catechisms, doctrines, and dogmas—general principles that never seem to catch the essence of human existence. No matter how well educated an Indian may become, he or she also suspects that Western culture is not an adequate representation of reality . . . the trick is somehow to relate what one feels with what one is taught to think. (1979)

Native knowledge has, from the onset of European Contact, been subjugated and devalued. This knowledge was in languages they didn't understand or want to understand—perhaps because getting to know the people of this hemisphere wasn't the objective. The objective was to conquer and exploit. One couldn't rightly do either if the Natives were considered humans with value and thought and creativity. The foundation was laid by the disregard for Indigenous people and their knowledge of the world and universe around them. But as Native Cherokee speaker and elder Tom Belt has said, "If you understand our language, by translation of even simple terms, one can easily see the 'science' of how the world works. For example, we say 'rooted in the mountains,' this conveys an understanding in English that we have longevity in the mountains, we are here to stay, and our roots go deep into the ground as trees' roots do. But in Cherokee, the word for root is *una sde tla* and the word for helping is *a sde l'da*." Tom continues:

Cherokees understanding about the word rooted is, "linguistically *a sde* and *sde tla* are common to each other and both are the same conceptually. The concept or idea exemplified by this comes from the same place—doing something to sustain. A root is a sustainer. It keeps life going. It has lots of tools and does lots of

things. It is a producer and consumer and is inextrica-
bly involved in the completion of a larger system of life,
one that communicates. Our language reflects the science—the knowledge of plant behavior. Our language
is verb based, polysynthetic language with active, ki-
netic concepts. Our language just doesn't label, but is
action oriented. The reason why it is verb based is that
is the way the world is interpreted—it is science talk.
(Tom Belt, pers. comm., Cullowhee, NC, 2018)

This translation of "rooted" is of particular interest to me as I
have had so many walks with elders in our region's forests where
plant and tree behaviors have been discussed. Cherokee elders Iva
Ratter, Onita Bush, Tom Belt, and others, along with my mom, who
was also knowledgeable about plants, have all made statements about
plants and/or trees, such as "they have moved this year—something
about where they were wasn't right for them" or "they will tell you
which one is the right one for use" or "they recognize you are here."
One elder who very rarely spoke at our Elders and Clinicians meetings spoke up quite clearly when we were talking about our relationship with trees. She said, "my father told me when I was a child to
not forget to go outside and hug this large oak tree we had in our
yard. He said to wrap my arms around it as far as they would go and
tell the tree thank you for shading us and keeping us safe; so every
morning on my way out to school, I would put my arms around that
tree and thank it for its purpose."

Daniel Chamovitz's (2017) *What a Plant Knows* sheds light on
these and other abilities of plants that reinforce the wisdom and understanding of these elders. He says, "Think about this: Plants see
you . . . Plants must be aware of the dynamic visual environment
around them in order to survive . . . Plants undoubtedly detect visible

(and invisible) electromagnetic waves." Chamovitz goes on to discuss the parallel similarities between plant and human biology and to describe how genetically more complex plants are than animals.

Furthering our understanding of the complex and symbiotic lives of trees, Peter Wohlleben has garnered tremendous international response from his book *Hidden Life of Trees: What They Feel, How They Communicate*. He opens up discussion for the Western scientific community to consider the communal relationships of trees, their ability to communicate, send messages, and take care of one another. These are all concepts that Indigenous people—and more specifically the Cherokees, who have lived in a temperate rainforest for centuries—have understood.

There are dozens of other examples, but to the Cherokee it represents the thousands of years of occupation in a region where close observation, trial and re-trial have taken place. For example, the "people of the earth," or Kituwah people, had language and knowledge of an unknown multitude of plants and their usages (in the hundreds and possibly thousands), as well as a cosmologic system that was mentioned by the earliest of travelers in their region, such as William Bartram (see Waselkov and Braund 1995, 145). Even Randolph, in his *British Travelers Among the Southern Indians, 1660–1763*, states, "The European considered native technology to be primitive, but the colonial white seldom attempted to understand the complex social organization and religious beliefs of the red man" (1973, 16–18),

This was the objective of colonization of Indigenous people: to use Christianization to justify and forward the economic and complete exploitation of Native people. As Milanich explains in his work *Laboring in the Fields of the Lord*, "Missions were colonialism. The missionary process was essential to the goal of colonialism: creating profits by manipulating the land and its people" (1999, xiii). There was no consideration of their value as human beings, just what they had and what they could do for the colonizers. For more robust and disgusting details of how that came down, I would suggest Bartolomé de las Casas's *In Defense of the Indians*, Robert Berkhofer's *Salvation and the Savage*, and David Stannard's *American Holocaust*, to start. For there to be an understanding of Native worldview, there had to be a willingness to value and apply their knowledge. This has continued to be problematic, as it causes continued misunderstanding and miscommunication between the dominant society and Natives today. As Vine Deloria put it:

> Western people don't have a problem—they don't seem concerned with the ultimate truth of what they are taught—Knowledge is correlated with a higher status employment . . . Indian customs and beliefs were regarded as primitive, superstitious, and unworthy of serious attention . . . So the question of the validity of knowledge contained in Indian traditions was eliminated before any discussions of reality began. (1979, viii)

Several years ago, Western Carolina University and the Center for Native Health hosted the first Native Science Dialogues on the US East Coast. Nine Native scientists came from almost as many Tribes to discuss the application of their epistemologies to the mission of a symposium we started at our university around 2010 called "Rooted in the Mountains: Valuing Our Common Ground." The intent of the symposium is to integrate Traditional Knowledge with health and environmental issues. In this initial meeting, the lead discussant was Dr. Leroy Little Bear (Blackfoot), who began these Dialogues with world renowned physicist Dr. David Bohm. After Dr. Bohm's passing in 1992, Dr. Little Bear continued discussions of quantum physics and metaphysics as they were related to Native Science or Traditional Knowledge. Little Bear works with a group of

Native elders, speakers, and scientists to discuss the interdisciplinary nature of TK.

In the Dialogues that took place on our campus, Diné elder Dr. David Begay commented on Native students in the academy. He said:

> American Indian students go to universities alone. No one understands them. They go through and get their degrees but can't apply them at home. Universities don't serve everybody or all of an individual—only a piece of their needs. You have to create a model of interdisciplinary work. The world of interrelationship means things don't happen on their own. Native people have a hard time thinking in a separated world. You must be able to process how the world is interconnected. English compartmentalizes stuff. It puts humans in the forefront, whereas most Native languages don't. The center of the language is nature, not man. Life must come first; the law of entropy means the land will restore itself. Go and ask elders regarding a process to manage renewal and they will say, look at nature with the daily, weekly, monthly, seasonal processes—they are all in nature."
>
> (David Begay, pers. comm., Cullowhee, NC, 2011)

One of the questions posited at this meeting by Dr. Little Bear was how to respond to the statement "When the land is sick, I am sick. And when I am sick the land is sick." Dr. Begay responded: "In Navajo, the word for land is *shekaya* which means the connection to earth under the moccasins. My mother is *shema*, which means like a mother and infant relationship. She, the root in each word, links the meaning together. This land is our mother earth, not just land or dirt, but the earth that has a bond with us like a mother does with her infant child. They are inseparable." Jim Rock (Dakota), a Native scientist also participating in the dialogues said, "The longest distance is often between the heart and mind. When we breathe in air, we are where space and earth meet. The breath goes out to the trees. We are all in space, not welcoming, but dark and cold—the breath, however, unites us all. Our heart beats and keeps us warm. Of course we are all connected, we all are to love each other as we love mother earth" (pers. comm., Cullowhee, NC, 2011).

These statements make tremendous sense to me as an Appalachian person, someone whose identity is synonymous with place. For most of us who grew up and identify with rural living, we try to make sense of the world by relating issues to what we know and have experienced in the natural world. I often read and reread the writings of Wendell Berry, agriculturalist and philosopher, who speaks to the notion much like that of Indigenous elders that the land protects and nurtures us as we have a responsibility to the land as well. As a lifelong farmer, Berry writes about food, diet, economics, and health, among other topics (see Berry 2002).

In *The Farm* (1995) he writes, "If you're going to deal with the issues of health in the modern world, you are going to have to deal with much absurdity . . . the modern medical industry faithfully imitates disease in the way it isolates us and parcels us out. If, for example, intense and persistent pain causes you to only pay attention to your stomach, then you must leave home, community, and family and go to a sometimes distant clinic or hospital where you will be cared for by a specialist who will only pay attention to your stomach . . . I believe that health is wholeness. For many years I have turned again and again to the work of English agriculturalist Sir Albert Howard who said in *The Soil and Health*, 'the whole problem of health in soil, plant, animal, and man, is one great subject'" (89–90). Berry goes on to say that "I believe that the community—in the fullest sense: a place and all its creatures—is the smallest unit of health and that to speak of the health of an isolated individual is a contradiction in terms" (ibid).

When speaking of Cherokee medicine, most people think of going into the mountains and gathering a plant to be used for healing a specific ailment. It is a much more complicated and sophisticated task. One must consider the larger contextual environment—this is critical in Cherokee medicinal practices. This is why so much caution is associated with protecting "sacred formulas." It is more to protect those who would use those formulas. Without knowing the language, understanding the time of day, month, week, season, which of many plants to choose, etc., more harm than good can occur.

Dr. Eduard Duran, a Native psychologist and pioneer of the "soul wound" model, prominent in counseling Native populations, addressed a group of Cherokee health providers and clinicians in 2010. He spoke of the responsibility of clinicians to integrate "Native ways of doing and thinking" in their service to Cherokee people. The western-trained health provider is taught to externally treat a patient. To rely upon medication, pills, and liquids that quickly take effect and treat illness is in large part missing the understanding of healing from the inside–out instead of from the outside–in, as Western medical professionals are taught. This is inclusive of Duran's notion that money-based, multi-national pharmaceutical corporations embrace a spirit that is counter-productive to the healing process—that using plants in the commercial fashion (in large volume) is in essence raping the land and the plants of their spirit and innate substance. There is no "relationship" and interconnectedness that imbues the spirit of healing.

We forget the healing spirit and protocols that respect the earth, plants, water, and other natural resources that provide us with healing and allow co-existence of other species. Instead, the spirit of exploitation is aligned with the pharmaceutical and medical industries.

This spirit may also be connected with the epidemic of over-production and distribution of opioids and other medications that have encouraged addiction and destruction of health.

As we reflect on our connection with the earth and all that is on it, we can easily find examples of how toxic dumps, coal and uranium mining, and polluted water make us sick. We also can understand through research regarding "psychoterratic distress" that there are serious consequences for rural people who witness the destruction and wholesale decimation of their land. Glenn Albrecht (2010) writes in his chapter "Solastalgia and the Creation of New Ways of Living" that depression, sadness, and consuming distress are "human responses to the lived experience of an emerging negative relationship to a home environment." Love for our land and strong identity with place is said to be part of an organic interconnection or, in the words of Carl Jung, an organic unity that reflects humans and their environment as a "single tissue." There are many languages that categorize the extreme unbalance people feel when their physical world changes rapidly, but English is not one of them.

The ancient knowledge of being connected to all else around us is being understood through the work of Native elders, speakers, scientists, and physicists. Today's technology reinforces the teachings of Indigenous people that we are all related as we are all made up of the same matter. We are swimming in constantly moving cells of energy that are influenced by our behaviors—and some say even our thoughts and tone of our voice. I was recently listening to an interview on National Public Radio with Dr. Jill Bolte Taylor, a neuroanatomist and national spokesperson for the Harvard Brain Tissue Resource Center. She spoke of her book *My Stroke of Insight* (2009) and discussed this notion of energy being emitted in all things around us. She said the brain is capable of tapping into and processing this activity at some level. She writes:

As information processing machines, our ability to process data about the external world begins at the level of
sensory perception. Although most of us are rarely aware
of it, our sensory receptors are designed to detect information at the energy level. Because everything around
us—the air we breathe, even the materials we use to build
with—are composed of spinning and vibrating atomic
particles, you and I are literally swimming in a turbulent
sea of electromagnetic fields. We are part of it. We are
enveloped within it, and through our sensory apparatus,
we experience what is. (18)

What came to mind when I heard this was that the universal Indigenous paradigm "we are all connected" is being proven by Western sciences, from neuroanatomy to quantum physics. We aren't
just all connected to one another, but every other living thing on
the planet—and in the universe! If we can begin to think more like
our Indigenous brothers and sisters, we might have a chance of eco-
logical and health renewal and a more effective understanding of
obtaining true wellness or as the Kituwah say *tohi'*.

Finally, we are seeing a breakthrough that hopefully will bring
together the sciences of Traditional Knowledge and the social and
biological sciences. As health professionals and others are working
to intervene in problems of stress, trauma, and chronic diseases,
these "sciences" are reflecting an interdisciplinary approach in understanding causality and treatment. Understanding culture is a
large part of this approach, and epigenetics is one example of this
intersection.

I hope that we find a common ground where those of us from
the colonizing dominant culture will reflect on these tenets of Native Science or TK that recognize we are in a relationship with all in

our world. As physicist David Bohm wrote, "The generic thought processes of humanity incline toward perceiving the world in a fragmentary way, breaking things up which are really not separate" (1996, xvi-xvii).

Works Cited

Albrecht, Glenn. 2010. "Solastalgia and the Creation of New Ways of Living." In *Nature and Culture: Rebuilding Lost Connections*, edited by Sarah Pilgrim and Jules N. Pretty, 207–234. London, UK: Earthscan.

Berkhofer, Robert F. 1976. *Salvation and the Savage: An Analysis of Protestant Missions and American Indian Response, 1787–1862*. New York: Atheneum.

Berry, Wendell. 2002. *The Art of the Commonplace: The Agrarian Essays of Wendell Berry*. Edited and introduced by Norman Wirzba. Washington, DC: Shoemaker and Hoard.

Berry, Wendell. 1995. *The Farm*. Monterey, KY: Larkspur Press.

Bohm, David. 1996. *On Dialogue*. New York: Routledge.

Bray, Warwick, ed. 1993. *The Meeting of Two Worlds: Europe and the Americas, 1492–1650*. Proceedings of the British Academy 81. New York: Oxford University Press.

Casas, Bartolomé de las. 1992. *In Defense of the Indians: The defense of the Most Reverend Lord, Don Fray Bartolomé de las Casas, of the Order of Preachers, late Bishop of Chiapa, against the persecutors and slanderers of the peoples of the New World discovered across the seas*. Translated, edited, and annotated by Stafford Poole. Dekalb: Northern Illinois University Press.

Chamovitz, Daniel. 2017. *What a Plant Knows: A Field Guide to the Senses*, rev. ed. New York: Scientific American/Farrar, Straus and Giroux.

Deloria, Vine. 1979. *Metaphysics of Modern Existence*. New York: Harper and Row.

Fedoroff, Nina V. 2003. "Prehistoric GM Corn," *Science* 302 (5648): 1158–1159. https://doi.org/10.1126/science.1092042.

Greenblatt, Stephen, ed. 1993. *New World Encounters*. Los Angeles: University of California Press.

Martin-Hill, Dawn. 2008. *The Lubicon Lake Nation: Indigenous Knowledge and Power*. Toronto: University of Toronto Press.

Milanich, Jerald T. 1999. *Laboring in the Fields of the Lord: Spanish Missions and Southeastern Indians*. Washington, DC: The Smithsonian Institution Press.

Randolph, J. Ralph. 1973. *British Travelers Among the Southern Indians, 1660–1763.* Norman: University of Oklahoma Press.

Stannard, David. 1992. *American Holocaust: Columbus and the Conquest of the New World.* New York: Oxford University Press.

Taylor, Jill Bolte. 2009. *My Stroke of Insight: A Brain Scientist's Personal Journey.* New York: Plume.

Veteto, James, Gary Paul Nabhan, Regina Fitzsimmons, Kanin Routson, and Deja Walker, eds. 2011. *Place-Based Foods of Appalachia: From Rarity to Community Restoration and Market Recovery,* Report available from *http://gpnabhan@email.arizona.edu.*

Waselkov, Gregory A. and Kathryn E. Holland Braund, eds. 1995. *William Bartram on the Southeastern Indians.* Lincoln: University of Nebraska Press.

Wohlleben, Peter. 2016. *The Hidden Life of Trees: What They Feel, How They Communicate—Discoveries from a Secret World.* Vancouver, Canada: Greystone Books.

About the Contributors

Trey Adcock (Cherokee Nation) obtained his PhD from the University of North Carolina at Chapel Hill, where he was awarded a Sequoyah Dissertation Fellowship in the Royster Society of Fellows. Currently, he is assistant professor in education and director of American Indian outreach at the University of North Carolina Asheville. At UNC Asheville he works directly with the American Indian student population as the faculty advisor for the Native American Student Association and serves on the Diversity Action Council for the university. He resides on a small farm in the mountains of Western North Carolina with his wife and two kids.

Raymond D. Fogelson, emeritus professor in the Departments of Anthropology, Comparative Human Development, Psychology, and the College at the University of Chicago, passed away on January 20, 2020. Professor Fogelson was widely recognized as a leading authority on Native American ethnology, with a specific focus on the Southeast. He conducted fieldwork with members of the Eastern Cherokee, Shuswap, and Oklahoma Cherokee and Creek communities. His expertise was wide-ranging, including the comparative studies of religion, psychological anthropology, museum anthropology, tourism, and hunting and gathering societies. He was a founding figure in the field of ethnohistory. After his retirement in 2011, the University of Chicago Master of Arts Program in the Social Sciences created the Raymond D. Fogelson Prize in his honor, for the highest distinction in the field of ethnology or history.

HARTWELL S. FRANCIS is currently the education curriculum developer for the Kituwah Preservation and Education Program of the Eastern Band of Cherokee Indians. In that role, he develops Cherokee-language content materials for pre-school and elementary immersion students and Cherokee-language education materials for the community. Francis is the founding director of the Western Carolina University Cherokee Language Program. He holds a PhD in theoretical linguistics from the University of Colorado, Boulder, and an MATESOL from Portland State University. His linguistics work includes a study of Arapaho verb structure. Francis has lived and worked in Mexico and Japan. His current focus of study includes content education in endangered languages, learning materials development in collaboration with speakers of endangered languages, and language attainment assessment for learners of endangered languages. He grew up in Albuquerque and Northern New Mexico.

LISA J. LEFLER is director of Western Carolina University's Culturally Based Native Health Programs, a collaborative program with the Eastern Band of Cherokee Indians and WCU's Colleges of Health and Human Sciences. The Native Health Certificate reflects a postcolonial model, involving Native communities from the ground up to educate health professionals regarding Native cultures in order to improve health care delivery for Native people. Lefler's other interests include Indian youth and addiction, diabetes, and health-related issues concerning stress, Native fatherhood, historic grief and trauma, and applying Native science to contemporary issues.

BRANDON D. LUNDY is an associate professor of anthropology and an associate director in the School of Conflict Management, Peacebuilding and Development at Kennesaw State University. He serves as the editor of the journal *Economic Anthropology* and as an associate editor for the *Journal of Peacebuilding and Development*. Receiving his PhDs from SUNY at Buffalo and the University of Science and Technology of Lille, France, Lundy's work focuses on sustainable livelihoods including food security, ethnoeconomics, transnational labor migration, and entrepreneurship. He is the editor or co-editor of five books including two on *Indigenous Conflict Management Strategies* and one on *Teaching Africa*. Lundy has served as a country specialist (Guinea-Bissau) for the US State Department and regularly presents nationally and internationally. After participating in a Fulbright-Hays in the summer of 2016 in Senegal on "Religion and Diversity in West Africa," he became a Fulbright Specialist.

ALEX O'NEILL earned her Bachelor of Science in anthropology from Kennesaw State University in December 2014. She assisted co-authors Lundy and Patterson with the economic anthropology research in Bissau, Guinea-Bissau, in the Spring of 2014. Their collaborative work has been published in several journals including *Economic Anthropology* and *Development in Practice*. While earning her degree, O'Neill served several semesters as president of the Student Anthropology Club and vice president of the Lambda Alpha national honor society for anthropology.

MARK PATTERSON is professor of geography at Kennesaw State University in Georgia and coordinator of the Environmental Studies Program and Degree and Certificate Programs in Geographic Information Sciences (GIS).

JIM SARBAUGH is an independent scholar. Sarbaugh worked for many decades with his friend, mentor, and colleague Willard Walker (emeritus professor of anthropology at Wesleyan University prior to his death) on a variety of topics regarding both the Eastern Band of Cherokee Indians and the Cherokee Nation.

www.ingramcontent.com/pod-product-compliance
Lightning Source LLC
Chambersburg PA
CBHW030654270326
41929CB00007B/360